Control Statements

CASE expression OF
    constant expression : statement
    sequence; |
    constant expression : statement

    sequence; |

    ...
    constant expression : statement
    sequence;
ELSE
    statement sequence;
END;

FOR variable := expression TO
    expression BY constant DO
    statement sequence;
END;

IF boolean expression THEN
    statement sequence;
ELSIF boolean expression THEN
    statement sequence;

...
ELSE
    statement sequence;
END;

LOOP
    statement sequence;
    EXIT;
    statement sequence;
END;

REPEAT
    statement sequence;
UNTIL boolean expression;

WHILE boolean expression DO
    statement sequence;
END;

WITH record variable DO
    statement sequence;
END;

Modula-2

A Seafarer's Manual & Shipyard Guide

Edward J. Joyce

*Foreword by Richard Ohran, Director,
Modula Research Institute*

Illustrations by Tom Sloan

Addison-Wesley Publishing Company
READING, MASSACHUSETTS · MENLO PARK, CALIFORNIA
DON MILLS, ONTARIO · WOKINGHAM, ENGLAND
AMSTERDAM · SYDNEY
SINGAPORE · TOKYO · MADRID · BOGOTÁ · SANTIAGO · SAN JUAN

Library of Congress Cataloging in Publication Data

Joyce, Edward J.
  Modula–2

  Bibliography: p.
  Includes index.
  1. Modula–2 (Computer program language)   I. Title.
QA76.73.M63J69   1985   001.64′24   84–28347
ISBN 0–201–11587–5

Second Printing, March 1986
ISBN 0–201–11587–5
BCDEF–HA–89876

To Judi

The author is grateful to the following publishers for permission to reprint material as follows:

Daimon Verlag for Lilith photograph. Reprinted from *Lilith die erste Eva*, by Siegmund Hurwitz. Copyright © 1980 by Daimon Verlag, AG.

E.C. Publications for *Mad* cover illustration. Reprinted from the April 1978 issue of *Mad* magazine. Copyright © 1978 by E.C. Publications, Inc.

Little, Brown and Company for excerpt from *The Soul of a New Machine*, by Tracy Kidder. Copyright © 1981 by John Tracy Kidder.

John Wiley & Sons for excerpts from *A History of Mathematics*, by Carl B. Boyer. Copyright © 1968 by John Wiley & Sons, Inc. Reprinted by permission of John Wiley & Sons, Inc.

John Wiley & Sons for excerpt from *Software Reliability*, by Glenford J. Myers. Copyright © 1976 by John Wiley & Sons, Inc. Reprinted by permission of John Wiley & Sons, Inc.

Ziff-Davis for excerpts from "The Making of Modula-2," by Edward J. Joyce. Reprinted from the April 3, 1984, issue of *PC* magazine. Copyright © 1984 by Ziff-Davis Publishing Co.

Foreword

*F*rom my impressions, computer users and programmers regard the selection of a programming language as similar to the selection of a second natural language, such as German, French, or Italian. People usually choose a second natural language based on factors such as how easy the language is to learn, historical areas of use, how widespread a particular language is, where they want to travel, how politically significant the users of the language are, and other reasons quite unrelated to the language's basic structure. Rarely are natural languages discussed and evaluated according to their primary purpose, which is *the expression of an idea* or *the communication of a thought.* Is German more succinct than French? Does English provide a better repertoire of symbolic terms (words) than Spanish? Is Latin less ambiguous than Greek? There is little interest in such subjects.

Analogous conversations also take place regarding programming languages: Is Pascal available on the IBM? Are there more programs written in FORTRAN? Does the management smile upon those who know LISP? Will Ada be popular? And so it goes. Seldom do people face the real issue, which is: Is language *A* better for the creation of efficient, readable, and debuggable programs than language *B*?

Ed Joyce focused upon this issue when he publicized, from an interview with Niklaus Wirth, the concept of regarding a programming language as a "notation" rather than as a language. He thereby identified the Modula programming notation as a tool for the creation of programs and emphasized the effectiveness of the tool, rather than its popularity, as a prime consideration in the choice of a programming language.

There is ample demonstration of how a specific notation can ease a task even when different notations must yield exactly the same result. For example, consider the problem of division when attempted in Roman-numeral notation rather than in the more efficient Arabic notation. Or consider the Occidental use of phonetically represented words for writing and printing versus the Oriental use of pictorial symbols. Each of these examples supports the idea that the means are more important than the end (unless, of course, you get the wrong results).

Those who have paid attention to the forms of computer languages recently have seen structured programming become the rage. Rebellion against the freewheeling looseness of BASIC has resulted in attempts to improve that language by adding enforced structure. When Niklaus Wirth wrote Pascal, the academic community in particular took the new language to its heart as the ideal teaching language. Other structured languages, such as C and Ada, have made strong inroads into corporate and governmental America, and an economical language with a quite different structure, Forth, continues to inspire a cultlike fanaticism among many of its adherents. None of these languages has, however, captured everyone's imagination.

Modula-2, which Wirth designed to be more all-purpose than Pascal, combines an economy of language and a modular structure that, I think, surpasses the competition. In this book, Ed Joyce presents Modula-2, the better notation for use in creating programs. It is not Joyce's first attempt to present Modula-2. Shortly after the unveiling of the language, he grasped its importance and published numerous articles on the subject. This text has given him the opportunity to deal with the subject much more comprehensively.

The reader is advised to weigh carefully the effectiveness of Modula-2, even though it may not yet be available for the computing engine of his or her choice or requirements. Even when Modula-2 is not available on the host computing engine, it will often be better than other languages as a documentation and problem-solving tool. After working out a clean solution in Modula-2, the programmer can always resort to whatever grubby programming system the hardware vendor offers for the final implementation. He or she should, however, call the vendor and demand a modern tool to work with.

Modula-2: A Seafarer's Manual and Shipyard Guide will convince many people that Modula-2 is that modern tool. The author's ongoing nautical metaphor serves him well for explaining the concepts in an unintimidating manner. Although some previous programming experience is assumed, the writing is so clear that an enthusiastic novice should do well. Joyce also combines fine writing with technical skill, a refreshing change from the many labored computer books that may be superb technically, but that are so dry as to make them hard to finish.

Richard Ohran

—Director of the Modula
  Research Institute

—President of The Modula
  Corporation

—Associate Professor of
  Computer Science at
  Brigham Young University

Preface

At one time this paragraph started with the statement, "This book is meant to help the reader learn the computer programming language Modula-2 . . ." Continuing from there, I planned to follow the well-trodden yet formidable path to technical enlightenment by sawing through the subject limb by limb, board by board, hoping that the individual pieces eventually lodged themselves in the reader's cerebral cortex.

But then I reflected on the years I've slaved and toiled to master a few bits and bytes of computer expertise; the times I resorted to chewing gum, caffeine, and stronger potions to maintain consciousness while perusing the tomes, *System Analysis in the Abysmal Language, Fifty Ways To Leave a Subroutine,* and *FORTRAN IV with What Have You and Why Not*; the times I cursed the user's manuals that must have been penned by the same author who writes the descriptions embossed on the sides of Goodyear tires; and the times I begged, bartered, and bought information from a computer guru who was not about to release an iota of know-how to a neophyte without first mandating the sacrifice of that neophyte's first-born child.

Upon contemplating my hard-earned experience, I finally concluded that there's got to be a better way. If you've got to cross technical crevasses and master foreign tongues to reach the mountaintop of computing Nirvana, then the load should at least be lightened through a relaxed approach. Spice up the subject with sidebars. Inject a humorous line here and there. Show that *serious* and *science* aren't synonymous. After all, strong medicine goes down easier with a smile.

And when was the last time you saw a computer smile? Of course, you can't remember. By the time programmers wade through the manuals and concordances of technical minutiae, nary a cranium cell remains with an indulgent disposition. The somber mood percolates to the electronic brains by design, heredity, or osmosis. Which explains why computers always seem to end up as villains crashing multi-billion-dollar space flights, shifting decimal points west on paychecks and triggering class A alerts at NORAD (North American Air Defense Command) when flocks of geese fly over the

Arctic. The software guiding the machinery traces its lineage to beleaguered parents.

So the cure to boosting computing morale lies not with pasting smiling faces on consoles, although it's been tried. No, we need to start at the point of conception—the programmer. Give the software jock a break by distilling a degree of humor and levity into the task of learning the ropes of programming. The net result may not book comedy clubs to standing-room-only crowds, but at least the spinster of programs will have known some warmth and wit during training.

With that perspective established, let me now spell out where these humble pages are going.

A programming language is to computers what a ship is to the sea. In the sea, ships of all shapes and sizes navigate the myriad waterways. Huge commercial liners laden with tons of cargo lumber across the vast oceans. Streamlined yachts, honed to slice through frothing breakers and gusting winds, race up and down the shorelines. Below the surface, submarines probe the deepest kingdoms presided over by fish and coral. Canoes, kayaks, and rafts complete the picture, skirting the inlets, streams, and bays that cannot accommodate the larger craft.

In the sea of computing, the transport vehicles that bedeck the waterways are the programming languages. COBOL and FORTRAN carry the bulk of commercial cargo between the continents, as they have for years. These venerable liners have recently been joined by Ada, which certain admirals predict will eventually dominate the shipping lanes.

Languages such as Pascal and C strive for clarity, systematic expression, and ease of operation. Sailors the world over swear by the seaworthiness of these hearty vessels. The designs of the ships are, however, more than a decade old and ripe for improvement.

The submarines of the computing sea—the assemblers, machine languages, and microcodes—probe the deepest recesses of the hardware. These boats navigate submerged channels, invisible to surface ships, that provide shortcuts to destinations. Unfortunately, the shortcuts weave between rocky reefs and treacherous shoals, which frequently wreak havoc on the journeys of inexperienced skippers.

Last, but not least, are the BASICs, APLs, Logos, and other special-purpose vessels designed for the peculiar environments of rivers, inlets, canals, and the like. These vessels are often the sole means of traveling a certain route. Beyond their home turf, however, they have difficulty negotiating the currents and tides of open water. A long cruise in this type of craft can be as uncomfortable as crossing the Pacific with Thor Heyerdahl in his balsa-wood raft, the *Kon Tiki*.

Where does the programming language Modula-2 fit in the sea of computing? Modula-2 resembles a sleek sailboat designed for elegance as well as practicality. In some respects, the language mirrors its older sibling, Pascal. On the other hand, a host of improvements in features, structure, and syntax distinguish it from its predecessor. Overall, Modula-2 maintains buoyancy in rough waters, even in straits and jetties unsuited for Pascal.

Although Modula-2 embodies simplicity in a structure of only forty reserved words, it stands ready to serve for virtually any type of sea duty. For ocean voyages, you can harness modules and pull the heaviest loads, tugboat style. The sleek design allows the language to negotiate the shallow harbors of the smallest computers. In addition, for probing beneath the surface, Modula-2 vessels carry miniature submarines, called *low-level facilities*, available for launching at a moment's notice.

This book is targeted at the venturesome sailor who would like to navigate the computing sea behind the helm of Modula-2. A working knowledge of one other language/ship will help when buzzwords of computerese surface in the prose without deference to landlubbers. The novice should not be discouraged, however, because eagerness to learn contributes as much to mastering Modula-2 as fluency in other computer languages does.

At its inception, Modula-2 was designed to operate the same across all the seven seas. In actual practice, it operates the same *most of the time*. Subtle distinctions exist between implementations owing to different hardware characteristics and individual interpretations of the language. These occur primarily in the low-level, system-dependent facilities and in the range of numeric variables. When these areas arise, I'll add emphasis to clarify nuances you may encounter on various computer systems.

The presentation followed in this book abides by the 10/90 rule, which stipulates that 10 percent of the people do 90 percent of the talking; 10 percent of the roads carry 90 percent of the traffic; and 10 percent of a computer language performs 90 percent of the work. Hence, the bulk of the text concentrates on that part of Modula-2's repertoire most frequently called to active duty.

The skewed approach doesn't mean that 90 percent of the language is ignored. On the contrary, the discriminating aficionado of computing dialects will find the entire vocabulary of Modula-2 covered by the final chapter.

The Modula-2 lessons presented are liberally sprinkled with program examples. At the beginning, the examples are complete, syntactically correct programs. After you've sampled a few of these full meals, you'll see that examples often appear as extracts of Modula-2 programs that highlight topics at hand. A series of three horizontal dots indicates the extracted form or program segment. For example,

```
VAR
   WindSpeed : CARDINAL;
   ...
   IF (WindSpeed > 100) THEN
      StayInPort;
   END;
```

means that the statements shown are an abridgment of a complete program.

Besides showing what works, I also show what doesn't work. Human intuition is a great fountain of knowledge. It pieces together the tiniest scraps of information and delivers them to the conscious mind in the form of a hunch. We're able to solve new problems based on some past, perhaps forgotten, related experience. Unfortunately, in programming these educated guesses occasionally miss their mark. What passes in English or even in another programming language may fizzle in Modula-2. Where such hazards crop up, I'll post warnings.

The seasoned Pascal skipper seeking a crash course in Modula-2 should begin with chapter seven. Modula-2 inherits the hull design pioneered by its predecessor, Pascal. Those who have cruised the sea behind the helm of Pascal will be able to get a good feel for Modula-2 by reading chapter seven, which highlights the exact differences between the two craft. From that point, you can proceed to other chapters for a comprehensive treatment of Modula-2 seafaring.

A problem section follows each chapter for those who desire self-study by free choice or academic coercion. The problems vary in length and difficulty. To help you make your selection in terms of your own time and experience, the problems are rated in four categories:

Leisure (L)   An easy problem that can be worked in your head while watching reruns of *Gilligan's Island.*

Moderate (M)   A more challenging problem that tests basic understanding of Modula-2. Requires a minimum three-minute commercial break.

Difficult (D)   A lengthy, nontrivial problem suitable for a term project. May cost you a few episodes of *Gilligan's Island.*

Strenuous (S)   A research project that has yet to be solved. Venturesome scholars may wish to apply for funding from the National Academy of Sciences and publish the results (if successful) in *Scientific American.*

During the year and a half in which I and my trusty computer had little else on our minds except Modula-2, I was asked almost daily by friends, relatives, and associates, "What is Modula-2?" This query was more often than not followed by, "Why write a book on Modula-2?" The former question is more than adequately covered, I hope, in the ensuing chapters. A precise reply to the latter question may lead to a dissertation on the motivation of the human spirit. Without going that far, however, it is enlightening to mention the individuals who played key roles in the development of this book.

The endeavor to understand and explain computers and programming languages depends on confidence in dealing with the abstract and analytical. The confidence that I have been able to muster owes to several teachers who over the years have patiently imparted their wisdom to a sometimes-recalcitrant student. Particularly helpful was David Brown, who as an assistant professor in the mathematics department at the University of Pittsburgh explained the mystery and magic of calculus. The best tribute I can think of comes from the student-class evaluation comments for the academic year 1970–1971: "Ounce for ounce, pound for pound, the best math prof is Dr. Brown."

I originally learned about Modula-2's potential for developing into the most significant programming language to date during a visit to the Modula Research Institute (MRI) in Provo, Utah. Director Richard Ohran spent hours demonstrating Modula-2 and the hardware engine designed for it, the Lilith computer. Richard claims that the Lilith is the fastest machine in the Rockies—followed closely by his Moto Guzzi motorcycle.

MRI staff members Rod Schiffman and Rod Riggs lent their technical acumen to help clarify operational aspects of certain Modula-2 constructs. They've also contributed significantly to Modula-2's spread in the computing community by designing a version of the Lilith compiler for personal computers that's priced at a nominal fee. Distributing that software falls into the bailiwick of Lyle Bingham, who, judging from the volume of mail at the local post office, must be the best-known celebrity in Provo.

If there's such a thing as a walking encyclopedia of Modula-2 literature, it resides in the body of A. Winsor Brown. Winsor can cite every speech, magazine article, conference paper, and piece of graffiti related to Modula-2 since the language was first conceived. When writing a book on Modula-2, you woo the friendship of Winsor in the same manner as you would court a spouse.

Finally, I appreciate the technical review of Cliff Zintgraff of Trinity University in San Antonio, Texas. Cliff didn't have to traipse across campus to some remote computer center to test the sample programs. He had only to decide which of three computers in his dorm room to put to the task. Talk about conspicuous consumption.

Before setting sail aboard Modula-2, let me borrow a few words from another scribe who once embarked on a similar journey.

> If any Errors have been committed in the Interpretation (as who in such Variety dare pretend to a full and perfect Understanding how, and in what sense every Author hath used a word) let Imbecility of Judgement, or Defect of Memory be pardoned, but zealous good will for propagating of Arts be encouraged, which was never more cordially designed than in this Work: but the performance is submitted to the Charity of thy Censure.

> —Joseph Moxon, *Mathematicks Made Easie*, 1700.

Bon voyage!

Contents

1
Introduction

1. Introduction

$\mathcal{T}$here's an old formula for writing called the five Ws: *Who, What, Where, When, and Why*. Read any book, newspaper column, or magazine article of substance, and it'll answer these fundamental questions about the subject matter.

The *Who, When, Why, and Where* of Modula-2 are questions of history. You may wonder what type of history could possibly lie behind a computer programming language. After all, computers are products of the twentieth century. How far back can a language trace its roots?

Certainly, somewhere short of Adam and Eve. Surprisingly, however, the roots span a few decades. Tracing the paths these roots took will help explain why in 1980, when the computing sea was teeming with more than 500 languages, Niklaus Wirth decided to launch yet another vessel into the milieu. The historical perspective also helps round out a functional understanding of the language and provides fertile fodder for saloon bets in Silicon Valley.

The main portion of the book delves into the remaining W, the *What* of Modula-2. In a pocket dictionary of computerese, Modula-2 might be defined as a compiled, high-level, structured language. Modula-2 shares the compiled trait with the languages COBOL, FORTRAN, Pascal, and C, to mention a few. Typically, two steps are involved in running a program written in one of these languages. First, the program, or *source code*, is compiled or translated into a machine form called *object code*; then the compiled or object program is executed.

Compiled languages stand in contrast to interpretive languages, such as BASIC, APL, and Forth. In these languages, the source statements are executed directly, without an intermediate compilation or translation step. Although interpretive languages eliminate the compilation step, they require considerably longer execution times.

Modula-2 is called a *high-level language* because it exhibits significant independence from the underlying machine architecture. The programmer doesn't need to know that the system stack is only eight layers deep or that the microprocessor runs on unleaded gasoline. The high-level trait insulates the programmer from the low-level operation of the hardware.

Finally, Modula-2 earns the title *structured* because it facilitates structured programming. You might ask, what is structured programming? Well, in defining structured programming, as in defining smooth whiskey, luxury yachts, and user friendliness, it's easier to say what it isn't than what it is.

Be that as it may, I'll go on record with a definition borrowed in part from the *Encyclopedia of Computer Science and Engineering*. Structured programming entails construction of programs from logical subunits that either are structured programs themselves or consist of a small number of particularly well-understood control structures. As a minimum, a structured language must have an if-then-else compound-decision statement and at least one form of iteration based on a boolean choice, namely, either do-while or repeat-until.

Another way of viewing structured programming is that it fosters an attitude of writing code with the intent of communicating with people as well as machines. Readability and ease of understanding characterize structured programs. Besides Modula-2, the languages Pascal, Ada, and C share the structured label because they embody structured-programming constructs.

The worst nonstructured programs exhibit spaghetti logic, that is, a convoluted bowl of paths and branches with no apparent beginning or end. The time required to decipher such programs exceeds the half life of strontium-90.

Polished programmers produce programs that exhibit the qualities of structure; namely, readability and minimal complexity, regardless of the language. They pursue their craft in the manner of the expert tailor who produces fine garments with needle and thread as well as with the sewing machine.

1.1 Modula-2's Roots

The evolution of Modula-2 lies embedded in the legacy of languages established over twenty-five years by Niklaus K. Wirth, the Swiss computer scientist of Pascal fame. The story begins in 1958 when Wirth, at twenty-four years of age, completed an electrical-engineering degree at the Swiss Federal Institute of Technology in Zurich. He then left his native Switzerland to pursue graduate study at Laval University in Quebec and the University of California at Berkeley.

While experimenting with circuit designs, Wirth came to realize that building hardware without a fundamental understanding of software and a precise knowledge of the ultimate computer application was like trying to build a canoe without ever having been in the water. He therefore temporarily abandoned hardware construction in favor of software development, a sojourn that eventually lasted twenty years.

The foray into software started right off in computer linguistics. Wirth and a group of colleagues wrote a compiler for a language dubbed Euler. Euler was an attempt to crystallize the fundamentals of languages such as Algol-60 into a working set as compact yet as universal as possible. Although Euler was experimental in nature and never achieved commercial success, it did whet Wirth's appetite for language design; it also simultaneously satisfied the requirements for a doctoral dissertation.

Upon completing the doctorate in 1963, Wirth departed Berkeley to join the budding computer science department of Stanford University, a prime location from which to watch the burgeoning computer technology of Silicon Valley. As an assistant professor at Stanford, he continued cultivating computer dialects. His next language, PL360, made its debut in 1965.

Gerald Weinberg, in *The Psychology of Computer Programming*, referred to the publication of PL360 as "one of the most important papers for the future of systems programming to come out in the last decade." PL360 imposed the advantages of block structure on the assembly language of the IBM 360 computer. At the same time, it conceptually controlled the code generated at the machine level.

Originally, Wirth designed PL360 as a tool for revising another language, Algol-60. He had the choice of writing the revised Algol-60 compiler in FORTRAN or assembly language. "Neither was very attractive so I wrote PL360 and implemented it as a kind of bootstrapping tool," recalled Wirth.

The project to revise Algol-60 was actually a joint effort between Wirth and the eminent English computer scientist Charles Anthony Hoare. They were invited by the International Federation for Information Processing (IFIP) to serve on a committee with the best-known language experts to develop a successor to Algol-60. Since its introduction in 1960, Algol-60, one of the first structured languages, had drawn a wide following especially in Europe.

Over a period of three years, Wirth and Hoare met with the committee to hammer out an improved Algol-60. Following each meeting, the draft of the language grew into a longer and thicker document as committee members tacked on their favorite bells and whistles. With each additional "feature," Wirth's disillusionment deepened, paralleling the mushrooming complexity of the language. Finally, in 1968, the "long-gestated monster" came to birth, as one committee member put it, and was christened Algol-68. Wirth and several colleagues submitted a minority report in protest.

The disagreements over Algol-68 reinforced Wirth's belief that the creation of a language is best accomplished under the firm intellectual grip of a single, unifying mind. This fundamental tenet still guides his work today, and he regularly turns down requests to serve on language committees.

Wirth's work on the IFIP committee did produce an offshoot of Algol-60 that was published in 1966 and subsequently entitled Algol-W by its many happy users. Algol-W produced effective programs by encouraging the programmer to express a problem explicitly, without unstated presuppositions. The language derived its power and flexibility from a unifying simplicity rather than from poorly integrated features and facilities. Those who have tasted the varieties of Algol will detect its flavor in Pascal and Modula-2. Hoare called it "an excellent language . . . a worthy successor to Algol-60 [as well as] a worthy predecessor of Pascal."

While the IFIP's committee continued to wrestle with Algol-68, Wirth returned to his native Switzerland after an eight-year absence, motivated by "the feeling that I really ought to have a decent structured language for doing what interests me—writing compilers and systems programs." Drawing on his accumulated experience and firm convictions about structured programming, he concocted "a clean language" that embodied "clean concepts for teaching." The result was a language called Pascal, named after the famous French mathematician who developed one of the first calculating machines in 1639.

Pascal was slow in catching on by today's standards. The first compiler came to life in 1970 on a Control Data Corporation mainframe computer. (Wirth practiced what he preached regarding the suitability of a high-level language for systems-level programming—he ultimately wrote the compiler in Pascal.) By 1977, the Pascal User's Group listed over 100 implementations, but most colleges and universities had yet to offer courses in Pascal, and the selection of textbooks was slim. Within that same year, though,

Pascal started scaling the charts when the University of California at San Diego (UCSD) began adapting Pascal systems for any microprocessor chip with forty legs.

Even with no commercial backing, Pascal succeeded on its own merits and propagated across hardware boundaries, ranging from the behemoth Cray-1 to the least expensive home computers. Professional programmers, who felt straitjacketed writing software for personal computers in BASIC, flocked to Pascal like typists forsaking Selectrics for word processors. Colleges and universities embraced Pascal as the quintessential dialect for instructing and illustrating computer logic, finding its clear and natural expression of algorithms and data structures a godsend for the classroom. In perhaps the strongest endorsement, the world's largest user of computers drafted Pascal as the basis for one of the most ambitious language projects of all time—the Department of Defense's new language, Ada, traces its lineage to Pascal.

"Pascal exceeded my wildest dreams," Wirth conceded. "I never had really thought about how popular it would be commercially. I had hopes it would find acceptance, particularly its ideas. Perhaps they would be incorporated into other developments. The fact that Pascal itself has been used so widely—that's a nice surprise."

Despite Pascal's popularity, it was far from a panacea. Critics complained that its inability to support separate compilation of modules hindered development of large programs. They cited the flawed CASE statement, which lacked an ELSE clause. They pointed out that the fixed size of arrays precluded the use of general-purpose math and string libraries. In another vein, FORTRAN and COBOL programmers, as well as assembly language coders—the high priests of a low cult—felt handcuffed by the compulsory declarations and detested Pascal for restraining them from moving data at whim amongst variables even if it meant shoehorning Moses Malone's foot into a size nine Nike hightop.

By the early 1980's this criticism crackled on the pages of industry journals, in articles such as "Real Programmers Don't Use Pascal," in which Wirth was called a quiche-eater. Wirth subsequently denied the accusation, citing his cheese-free diet.

Several times Wirth was asked to head up an effort to update Pascal, but a fresh approach was more in line with his personal philosophy. "If a language proves to be only marginally suitable for some application that was obviously not envisaged by its originator," he wrote in *Software— Practice and Experience*, "we should muster the courage to build a new, truly adequate tool, instead of just grafting a fix onto the existing one."

While universities, software houses, and computer companies were enhancing Pascal to suit their own particular needs, Wirth's interests gravitated to multiprogramming, the concurrent execution of several activities. To conduct experimentation and express multiprogramming primitives, he contrived a rudimentary language, Modula (without a suffix), which stands for *MODU*lar *LA*nguage. "Modula was never intended to be a language on the same level as Pascal," Wirth explained. "It contained primitives for multiprogramming plus as few other things as possible. Since writing a compiler is a lot of work, you don't want to carry any extra luggage in the language."

After mulling over the insight gained in experimenting with Modula, Wirth departed in 1976 for a year's sabbatical leave at the Xerox Palo Alto Research Center (PARC). At PARC, he hobnobbed with the architects of the Xerox Alto prototype computer and studied the Mesa language. The sophisticated graphics, mouse, and other concepts pioneered in the Alto later turned up in the Xerox Star and Apple Macintosh computers.

When Wirth left PARC, the creative juices were flowing full force with ideas for both hardware and software. He merged the bloodlines of Pascal, Modula, and Mesa to produce Modula-2. Then he reversed the industry axiom of writing software to fit existing computer hardware and designed a computer called the Lilith for Modula-2.

Wirth named his Modula-2 computer after Lilith, a demon in Jewish mythology who steals men away from their wives and children.

Today, Modula-2 has been implemented on a variety of computers, including the DEC VAX, IBM PC, Sage, Apple II, Macintosh, and Lisa. It is recognized as the Swiss army knife of languages, a universal tool that packs utility, simplicity, and economy in a streamlined case. It allows the programmer to focus on solving the problem at hand rather than grappling with a cornucopia of operators and struggling through a jungle of inconsistent syntax. The language's success is guaranteed by an unspoken, but implied, hallmark that accompanies its name. Like "Walkman by Sony" or "Color by Kodak," it's "Modula-2 by Wirth."

THE MAESTRO OF MODULA-2

On November 12, 1982, Ronald Reagan addressed a letter to 20 computer scientists and engineers. "I am delighted to extend my heartfelt congratulations," began the president, "to the pioneers who have become members of the Computer Industry Hall of Fame."

The list of Hall of Famers spanned the industry from head to toe, from Thomas Watson, Sr., the grand-patriarch of IBM, to Bill Gates, the guru of Microsoft, to Steve Jobs, the rootstock of Apple. Although the computing community could readily identify most of these inventors and innovators because of the landmark discoveries in electronics or corporate entities that bore their names, one academician stood out more for obscurity than notoriety. Niklaus K. Wirth holds no patents in silicon circuitry, never entrepreneured a high-tech firm, and isn't even a citizen of this country. His claim to fame rests in slim scholarly reports brimming with Greek symbols and esoteric mathematical notation. Over the past twenty years, these

reports have defined no fewer than five programming languages, cul-
minating with Modula-2 and earning the Swiss professor the title of
"Father of Structured Languages."

Ironically, the master of computer linguistics doesn't regard a programming language as a "language" at all. He shies away from the
popular notion of viewing a language as a medium of communication between human and machine. Rather, he sees it as an abstract
tool for the construction of computing machinery. "In my opinion,"
says Wirth, "*programming language* is ill-chosen and misleading.
Program notation would be eminently more appropriate."

However you care to define languages, there's no question that
Wirth knows them well. The grammars he has designed, published,
and implemented are milestones in the field of computer science. In
recognition of these accomplishments, the Institute of Electrical and
Electronics Engineers (IEEE) in 1983 bestowed on him their presti-
gious Emanuel R. Piore award and the York University in England
and the Institute of Technology in Lausanne, Switzerland, have con-
ferred honorary doctorates. Most recently, the Association for Computing Machinery honored Wirth with its 1984 Turing award for
outstanding technical contributions to computer science.

The 51-year-old professor could, in the words of one close associate, "spend all his time globetrotting around the world collecting ku-
dos," but he prefers the laboratories of the Swiss Federal Institute of
Technology (called ETH, Eidgenössische Technische Hochschule) in
Zurich where he hammers out the picks, shovels, and hoes of software cultivation.

Wirth's passion for design had its roots on the hardware side of
the fence early on. As a boy, he built remote-control model airplanes
from kits. After one particularly frustrating out-of-box failure, he decided to design and construct his own control unit. This hobbyist-
tinkering fostered an interest in electronics which led to an electrical
engineering degree in 1958 at ETH.

Reflecting on his early dabbling in electronics, Wirth said in a
tone of nostalgia, "Nowadays, most people get a working model of
anything by going to the store and buying it. In the past, everyone
knew that with a little creativity and effort you could build a better
product than those sold in stores. This was a great motivation to do
design work. The current trend of relying solely on shelf-products
has unfortunate implications for the future of software design, a
field in which nothing can replace a creative person's way of think-
ing."

Looking to the future of software, Wirth believes that the most significant advances will come from people, not tools. "I don't think we should expect gigantic strides through new tools," he contends. "The ultimate improvement will stem from better discipline and higher professional standards."

Figure 1–1 shows the date of first publication of prominent programming languages. Wirth's languages (shown in bold face) stand out as milestones in computer linguistics.

1.2 First Launch

Learning to pilot Modula-2, or any programming language, for that matter, is a hands-on proposition. You learn by seating yourself behind the wheel, charting a course, and easing into the current. Careful study of successful voyages, though, streamlines the educational process immensely.

| 1956 | 1960 | 1964 | 1968 | 1972 | 1976 | 1980 | 1984 |

MODULA-2 (*MODU*lar *LA*nguage 2)

ADA

MODULA (*MODU*lar *LA*nguage)

C (successor to B)

FORTH

LOGO

PASCAL

ALGOL-W

PL360 (*Programming* Language for the *360*)

PL/I (*Programming* Language One)

BASIC (*Beginner's All* purpose *Symbolic* Instruction *Code*)

APL (*A* Programming *Language*)

LISP (*LIS*t Processing)

ALGOL-60 (*ALGO*rithmic Language)

COBOL (*CO*mmon Business Oriented Language)

FORTRAN (*FOR*mula *TRAN*slation)

| 1956 | 1960 | 1964 | 1968 | 1972 | 1976 | 1980 | 1984 |

Figure 1—1

Program 1–1 introduces the first such voyage, a simple program that displays two phrases on the terminal screen. This program should execute as-is on any computer system with a Modula-2 compiler. Let's dissect the anatomy of this 12-line program to point out fundamental Modula-2 components.

Program 1–1 FirstLaunch

```
MODULE FirstLaunch;      (* Sample display program *)

FROM InOut IMPORT WriteLn,
                  WriteString;

BEGIN
   WriteLn;
   WriteString("Sitting on the dock of the bay, ");
   WriteLn;
   WriteLn;
   WriteString("Watching the tide roll away ... ");
   WriteLn;

END FirstLaunch.
```

The first line, the MODULE statement, designates the module name, FirstLaunch. Modules are the building blocks of Modula-2. Programs may consist of only one module, as this one does, or they may consist of several modules, including those borrowed from the *module library.*

The second part of the first line is bracketed by *comment delimiters.* Specifically, (*, an open parenthesis followed by an asterisk, indicates the beginning of the comment. The end of the comment is indicated by *), an asterisk followed by a closed parenthesis. Comments are used to add descriptive text to explain a program. They do not contain executable statements. They may also be used to designate compiler options on some systems.

Other examples of comments are

```
(* This program calculates the equations (90.0 − 32.0)/1.8 and
         (32.22*1.8) + 32 *)
WriteLn;    (* skip a line *)
WriteLn;    (* Skip a line so the text is uncluttered! *)
```

Comments may extend on multiple lines, and any characters, including arithmetic symbols and punctuation marks, may be part of a comment field.

The FROM statement in Program 1–1 *imports procedures* from another module so that they may be used within the current program. A *procedure* is a collection of instructions that perform a particular action. In this case, the procedures WriteLn and WriteString are imported from the module InOut. WriteLn writes a new line sequence on the terminal screen. (Note to Pascal skippers: Modula-2's WriteLn operates differently than its Pascal counterpart.) On most terminals the new line sequence consists of a carriage return and line feed. WriteString displays a string of characters.

InOut, by the way, is a library module common to all Modula-2 compilers. Appendix B lists the standard module library inherent to Modula-2 systems.

The process of importing procedures is like that of using prefinished products when building a sailboat. Theoretically, you could build a sailboat completely from scratch using a hammer, saw, nails, and raw lumber. To save time and labor, though, you'll probably piece parts of the boat together from prefinished components. The prefinished components typically include canvas sails, aluminum masts, glass portholes, galley cupboards, and other items common to all sailboats and available at shipyards. In Modula-2, the supply shipyard is the module library, which contains prefinished, commonly used procedures.

The last statement of the module, END, combines with the BEGIN statement to designate the start and finish of the *module body*. The instructions within the body are executed sequentially. In this simple program, the module body consists of WriteLn and WriteString procedure calls. The latter displays a string on the terminal screen. A *string* is any sequence of characters enclosed in double quotation marks. Examples of strings in WriteString statements are

    WriteString("Enter date in the format, MM/DD/YY");

which displays

    Enter date in the format, MM/DD/YY

and

    WriteString("Example: -----> 9/14/85 <-----");

which displays

    Example: -----> 9/14/85 <-----

Strings may also be enclosed by single quotation marks or apostrophes. This option allows double quotation marks to be embedded in a string. For example,

    WriteString('Enter date in the format, "MM/DD/YY" ');

displays

    Enter date in the format, "MM/DD/YY"

Finally, notice that each statement, except BEGIN and END, terminates with a semicolon. The semicolon serves as a *statement separator*. Although the program FirstLaunch has only one statement per line, the semicolon could be used to place multiple statements on a line.

    WriteLn;
    WriteString("Sitting on the dock of the bay");

is equivalent to

    WriteLn; WriteString("Sitting on the dock of the bay");

Placing multiple statements on a line, although syntactically acceptable, detracts from readability and consequently violates what are referred to as *standard conventions.* Standard conventions enable the program to be understood not only by the computer but also by other software jocks who may eventually follow in the footsteps of the program's author. What happens to careless coders who deviate from standard conventions? The penalty was established more than ten years ago:

> Programmers who fail to comply with the standard naming, formatting or commenting conventions should be forced to walk the plank. If it so happens that no plank is available, then they are to be politely requested to recode their programs in adherence to the standards.
>
> —inspired by Michael Spier, *The Typeset-10 Codex Programaticus. Technical Report* (Maynard, MA: Digital Equipment Corp., 1974).

If you should witness a violation of the standard conventions, you are urged to immediately call Crime Stoppers, the Association for Computing Machinery, or your local office of the Software Engineering Police.

1.3 Summary/Problems

Niklaus Wirth launched the programming language Modula-2 after studying Pascal's shortcomings for ten years. Modula-2 is a high-level, structured language distinguished by simple constructs and elegance of expression.

The core vocabulary of Modula-2 is extended by module libraries. These libraries handle input, output, and elementary mathematical operations. Libraries may also be augmented to suit particular applications. A statistical library, for example, might contain procedures to calculate correlation coefficients and averages. Importing a procedure from a library saves the programmer from having to reinvent the wheel.

Problems

1. [L] Which of the following are valid strings?
   a. "12 34 56 78 90"
   b. "2*a = 2*b + 2*c"
   c. ' "Aye, aye skipper!!!" '
   d. "The first mate said, 'Aye, aye' "
   e. "12 34 56 78 90'

2. [M] What results will the following program produce?

```
MODULE Sample;
(* Sample display program
FROM InOut IMPORT WriteString;
BEGIN
   WriteString("Sitting in the evening sun");
END Sample.      That's all! *)
```

3. [D] Modula-2 shares its roots with a language recently developed by the world's largest user of computers. This language was once known as strawman, woodenman, tinman, ironman, steelman, and green. What is it called now? In what ways is this language similar to Modula-2? In what ways does it differ?

2
Nautical Fundamentals

2. Nautical Fundamentals

The fundamental grammar of Modula-2—and of any programming language, for that matter—consists of the data, expressions, operators, and rules of protocol and syntax that congeal the distinct parts into living programs. For a group of Modula-2 statements to make sense, they must be organized within the framework of the prescribed grammar. Trying to understand Modula-2 statements that are inconsistent with the grammar makes no more sense than trying to interpret the sequential listing of words in the English dictionary as an essay.

2.1 Data

"Programs are composed of data and instructions." I can still hear Professor Conner making that statement on the first day of my introductory computer science course at the University of Pittsburgh. In more than ten years of weaving programs at a keyboard, I've yet to find an exception to that fundamental tenet. His next statement, unfortunately, doesn't ring so true: "Instructions act on data to produce meaningful results." I've had programs produce no results, too many results, and results that are yet to be deciphered. In any case, the spirit of the good professor's statement stands: instructions *should* act on data to produce meaningful results.

21

Data in Modula-2 falls into two categories: *variables* and *constants*. The main difference between the two is that the values of constants do not change during a program's execution. Variables, on the other hand, can run the gamut within a specified range of values.

Modula-2 requires explicit declarations of data. In other words, each data variable and constant must be explicitly specified before it is used. Declaration occurs in the variable and constant sections of the program, which are labeled appropriately VAR and CONST. For example, consider Program 2–1, which converts fathoms to inches. This program reads a numeric value (the number of fathoms) from the terminal keyboard, converts it to inches, and displays the result.

Program 2–1 Fathoms

```
MODULE Fathoms;      (* Convert fathoms to inches *)
FROM InOut IMPORT WriteLn,
                  WriteString,
                  WriteInt,
                  ReadInt;

CONST
   FeetInFathom = 6;
   InchesInFoot = 12;
   InchesInFathom = FeetInFathom * InchesInFoot;

VAR
   NumFathoms,
   TotalInches : INTEGER;

BEGIN
   WriteString("Enter number of fathoms: ");
   ReadInt(NumFathoms);
   TotalInches := NumFathoms * InchesInFathom;
   WriteLn;
   WriteInt(TotalInches,5);
   WriteLn;

END Fathoms.
```

The two main characteristics of variables and constants are their *names* and *types*. Names, such as NumFathoms and TotalInches, are designated by *identifiers*, as are modules and procedures. An identifier in

Modula-2 is defined as a sequence of letters and digits in which the first character must be a letter. Examples of valid identifiers are

```
FirstLaunch
WriteLn
Form1040
Z80register
pagecounter
PostOfficeBox
```

Invalid identifiers include

```
8087interface
page-counter
CP/M
End_Switch
MS DOS
user's
```

The first invalid identifier violates the criteria for an identifier because it does not begin with a letter. The second contains an illegal character, a dash. The third, fourth, fifth, and sixth also contain illegal characters: a slash, an underscore, a space, and an apostrophe, respectively.

Identifiers are case-sensitive; lower case is distinguished from upper case. Thus, pagecounter is considered to be distinct from PageCounter, which is considered to be distinct from PAGECOUNTER.

The only other restriction on identifiers is that reserved words must not be chosen as identifiers. Reserved words are words that have predesignated meanings in Modula-2. Some of these, such as MODULE, BEGIN, and END, have already been mentioned. The complete list appears in Appendix A.1.

Modula-2's reserved words are always written in upper case. Programmer-named identifiers *by convention* are written in lower case or in a combination of upper-and lower-case letters. (For the consequences of violating conventions, see page 17.)

Directly opposite the identifier of a constant declaration stands the constant expression. Constant expressions take many forms. The sample program Fathoms declared three constants; two were numeric values and one was a numeric expression. Constant expressions may also be strings, such as

```
CONST
  Reply = "Aye, Aye";
```

2.2 INTEGER *Numbers*

If you regard a variable as a two-sided object separated by a colon, the left side is occupied by the identifier name as just described. On the right side appears the *type characteristic*. It determines the values that a variable or constant may assume and the operations that may be performed with those values. In the sample program Fathoms, the variables NumFathoms and TotalInches are declared as type INTEGER.

The type INTEGER is used in its everyday sense. Integer variables denote whole numbers—positive, negative, or zero, without decimal points or fractional parts. Examples of integer and noninteger values are

integer	*noninteger*
2	1.5
136	136.
+8	+0.2
0	.01
−12345	−12.34

The range of Modula-2 integers may vary on different computer systems. On microcomputers, integers generally range from −32,768 to +32,767.

To determine the actual range of integers on any computer, you can invoke the procedures MIN and MAX. For example, the statements

```
VAR
   SmallInt,
   BigInt : INTEGER;
. . .
   SmallInt := MIN(INTEGER);
   BigInt := MAX(INTEGER);
```

assign the smallest and largest integer values to variables SmallInt and BigInt. MIN and MAX are *standard function procedures*, which determine the minimum and maximum values of a type. For all practical purposes, function procedures are the same as regular procedures except that they yield a value in an expression instead of performing an action as a stand-alone statement. MIN and MAX are called standard because they are integral to the language and, unlike procedures WriteLn and WriteString, need not be imported from a library module.

The previous example shows only part of a program. The program is obviously incomplete, because it lacks MODULE, BEGIN, and END statements. This abbreviated form is often used to focus on certain topics without writing out a complete program. The series of three horizontal dots indicates that the statements are an excerpt of a program as opposed to a complete model.

The symbol := in the previous program segment represents the *assignment operator*. Assignment in Modula-2 translates to the English words *takes on* or *becomes*. The statement x := 67; means that variable x takes on the value 67.

The assignment operator should not be confused with the equal sign (=) which has an entirely different interpretation. In constant declarations, for example, the equal sign has the same meaning as the English words *is the same as*. The declaration

```
CONST
   FeetInFathom = 6;
```

means that the constant identifier FeetInFathom is the same as the value six. Thus, the statement

```
NumFeet := NumFathoms * FeetInFathom;
```

is equivalent to

```
NumFeet := NumFathoms * 6;
```

For arithmetic calculations, five operators apply to variables and values of type INTEGER:

+	addition
−	subtraction
*	multiplication
DIV	integer division
MOD	remainder of integer division

The first three operators mirror their algebraic counterparts. DIV represents integer division, which always yields an integer result. Specifically, the statement

```
q := x DIV y;
```

means that variable q is assigned the value of the truncated quotient of dividing x by y. The remainder of a DIV operation, if any, is ignored and no rounding occurs.

For instance, the statements

```
VAR
   a,
   b,
   c : INTEGER;
. . .
a := 5 DIV 2;
b := 3 DIV 4;
c := 19 DIV (−10);
      (* negative divisors must be enclosed by parentheses *)
```

yield

variable	*contents*
a	2
b	0
c	−1

The last arithmetic operator associated with integers is the MOD, or modulus, operator. MOD signifies the remainder of integer division.

```
r := x MOD y;
```

means variable r is assigned the value of the remainder of dividing x by y. In the Modula-2 language, the MOD operator is valid only for positive x and y.

The statements

```
VAR
   a,
   b,
   c : INTEGER;
. . .
a := 5 MOD 2;
b := 3 MOD 4;
c := 248 MOD 248;
```

yield

variable	*contents*
a	1
b	3
c	0

Algebraically, the DIV and MOD operators can be expressed in the equations:

given

```
quotient := x DIV y;
remainder := x MOD y;
```

then the following are true:

```
x = (quotient * y) + remainder
0 <= remainder
remainder < ABS(y)
```

ABS stands for the absolute-value function. Notice that variable y must not be equal to zero, because division by zero is undefined.

LILAVATI, BOOK AND DAUGHTER

Prior to the twelfth century, mathematicians hadn't truly defined division by zero. It was Bhaskara of India (1114–ca. 1185) who first gave the modern-day definition of division by the "cipher." Bhaskara wrote,

Statement: Dividend 3. Divisor 0. Quotient the fraction 3/0. This fraction, of which the denominator is the cipher, is termed an infinite quantity. In this quantity consisting of that which has cipher for a divisor, there is no alteration, though many may be inserted or extracted; as no change takes place in the infinite and immutable God.

Bhaskara's best-known treatise on mathematics is *Lilavati*, a book he named after his daughter. According to legend, Lilavati lost the opportunity to marry because of her father's confidence in his astrological predictions. Bhaskara had calculated that his daughter might propitiously marry only once at one particular hour on a given day. On what was to have been her wedding day the eager bride was bending over the water clock. As the hour for the marriage approached, a pearl from her headdress fell, quite unnoticed, and stopped the outflow of water. Before the mishap was noted the propitious hour had passed. To console the unhappy girl, the father gave her name to his book on mathematics.

—Carl B. Boyer, *A History of Mathematics*, 1968.

Program 2–2, which illustrates the use of integer variables, displays the results of the arithmetic operations with integer values. The displayed results of this program are:

29   21   100   6   1

Program 2–2 SampleInt

```
MODULE SampleInt;      (* Demonstrate integer arithmetic *)

FROM InOut IMPORT WriteLn,
                  WriteInt;

VAR
    IaddResult,
    IsubResult,
    ImulResult,
    IdivResult,
    ImodResult : INTEGER;

BEGIN
    IaddResult := 25 + 4;
    IsubResult := 25 − 4;
    ImulResult := 25 * 4;
    IdivResult := 25 DIV 4;
    ImodResult := 25 MOD 4;
    WriteLn;
    WriteInt(IaddResult,5);
    WriteInt(IsubResult,5);
    WriteInt(ImulResult,5);
    WriteInt(IdivResult,5);
    WriteInt(ImodResult,5);
    WriteLn;

END SampleInt.
```

Integer Output

The procedure WriteInt in Program 2–2 is a cousin to WriteString. They both live in the module InOut. WriteInt displays INTEGER values on the terminal screen. Because INTEGER values are not stored internally in displayable or printable format, WriteInt converts the value to displayable ASCII (American Standard Code for Information Interchange) format before displaying it.

The general format for WriteInt is

WriteInt(i,n);

where i is an INTEGER and n specifies the field width of the displayed value. If the field width is greater than the number of significant digits in the value, the leading positions are filled with spaces. For example, the statements

```
WriteInt(8417,5);
WriteInt(63,5);
```

display " 8417" and "   63".

If the field width is zero, only the significant digits of the integer are displayed.

```
WriteInt(0803,0);      yields      "803"
```

and

```
WriteInt(−17,0);       yields      "−17"
```

If the integer exceeds the field size, all of the significant digits of the integer are displayed despite the field size. For example,

```
b := 1234;
WriteInt(b,2);
```

displays "1234" even though only a two-character field size is specified.

Another new concept can be exemplified by the program Fathoms (Program 2–1). Besides WriteString, the program employs one other procedure for accessing the terminal. The statement ReadInt(NumFathoms) reads an integer value from the terminal keyboard and places it in the variable NumFathoms.

In the Fathoms program, we saw that the type of a variable is specified when it is declared. No such specification follows constant declarations. How does Modula-2 determine the types of such constants? This is accomplished by inspecting the constant value. In the Fathoms program, the values six and 12 are both integers, therefore the constants FeetInFathom and InchesInFoot are treated as integers.

The third constant, InchesInFathom, is an *expression*. It is regarded as an integer because it is formed by multiplying two integer constants.

Generally speaking, an *expression* is composed of several *operands* and *operators*. An *operand* is a variable or constant designated by an identifier; an *operator* is a symbol specifying a particular action on the operands. For example, the symbols "+" (plus) and "−" (minus) are operators that perform arithmetic actions.

If there is any doubt as to how an expression will be evaluated, parentheses should be inserted to clarify the precedence of operations. The parts of the expression within the innermost parentheses are evaluated first. For example,

```
2 * ((3 * 4) + 5)
```

yields 34.

If parentheses are missing from an expression with multiple operators, the evaluation of the operators follows a default *precedence order*. The default precedence of operators is listed in Appendix A.1 for reference purposes. Because operator precedence varies from one computer language to the next, writing expressions based on default precedence inevitably leads to confusion. Parentheses should always be used to spell out the precedence of operators in a positive, nonambiguous fashion.

The program Fathoms also includes the *assignment operator*, :=. Variables must be assigned only values of the *same type*. In other words, it would be *illegal* in the program Fathoms to write

```
TotalInches := 12.41;
```

because 12.41 is not an integer value.

The assignment operator consists of two characters, the colon and equal sign, and is therefore called a *compound symbol*. Compound symbols must always appear without intervening spaces.

The same rule regarding spaces applies to reserved words, identifiers, and other compound symbols, such as the comment delimiters, (* and *). Modula-2 compares to a degree with English in this respect. For example, in English the word *orate* is not the same as the words *or ate*, nor is *forage* the same as *for age*. Similarly, in Modula-2, WriteString is distinct from Write String and BEGIN from BE GIN. Intervening spaces change the meanings of these items.

Spaces can be freely interspersed, however, between statements and operators. For example,

```
x := 67;
```

is interpreted the same as

```
x      :=      67;
```

and

```
x

   :=

          67     ;
```

Judicious use of this free format improves the style of a program, making it easier to read and understand.

Clearly,

```
TotalInches := NumFathoms * InchesInFathom;
WriteLn;
WriteInt(TotalInches,5);
```

is much easier to read than

```
TotalInches:=NumFathoms*InchesInFathom; WriteLn; WriteInt
(TotalInches,5);
```

although both are syntactically correct.

2.3 CARDINAL *Numbers*

Besides INTEGER, another type that can be used to declare whole numbers is CARDINAL. Type CARDINAL is identical to type INTEGER except that negative numbers are excluded. CARDINAL variables denote whole positive numbers or zero without decimal points or fractional parts. Examples of cardinal and non-cardinal values are

cardinal	non-cardinal
2	−2
136	1.5
+8	8.67
0	+0.2

The range of cardinal numbers may vary on different computer systems. On microcomputers, cardinal numbers generally range from 0 to +65,535.

Type CARDINAL offers two advantages over INTEGER. First, it covers a larger positive range, typically twice that of integers. Second, the computer processes numbers with positive-only values more efficiently.

The arithmetic operators associated with type INTEGER apply to type CARDINAL, namely,

+	addition
−	subtraction
*	multiplication
DIV	integer division
MOD	remainder of integer division

The main reason for mandating a type declaration with a variable is to prevent the variable from being inadvertently used in incompatible operations. Modula-2 ensures that CARDINAL and INTEGER variables are restricted to calculations with compatible variables, which usually means variables of the same type. If variables a, b, and c are defined as

```
VAR
    a,
    b : INTEGER;
    c : CARDINAL;
```

it is *illegal* to write

```
a := b * c;
```

because the types of the variables do not agree. In general, variables and constants of different types cannot be mixed in expressions and statements.

One exception to this rule is that INTEGER and CARDINAL variables are *assignment-compatible*. That is, integers can be assigned cardinal values and vice versa. Thus, in the previous example, it is valid to write

```
a := c;
c := b;
```

2.4 REAL *Numbers*

Although integer and cardinal variables are useful for applications such as counting, many numbers contain fractional parts or exceed 65,535. Modula-2's type REAL is made to order for these kinds of numbers.

Expression of REAL numbers requires a decimal point. Examples of real and nonreal values are

real	*nonreal*
1.	1
8.675	8
−12.34	−12345
0.0	0
0.	.0
+0.2	+2
0.2	.2

Notice that real value expressions in Modula-2 require at least one digit before the decimal point but do not require a digit following it.

Real values may also be expressed with a scale factor in *exponential*, or *power-of-ten*, notation. This notation is commonly used to represent very large or small quantities. Exponential notation is particularly useful to scientists who are trying to measure the size of the universe or to economists who are trying to calculate the federal budget deficit.

In general, exponential notation takes the form

±x.xxxxxxxEspp

where ±x.xxxxxx is a decimal number between ±1.0000000 and ±9.9999999, *E* stands for *exponentiation*, *s* is the sign of the power (absent or plus for positive, minus for negative), and *pp* is the exponent, or power, that indicates how many places the decimal point is to be shifted. If the sign of the power is positive, the decimal point is to be moved to the right; if negative, the decimal point is to be moved to the left.

For example, the speed of light is 186,000 miles per second. In exponential notation this can be expressed as 1.86E5. Exponential notation is useful when expressing very large numbers:

4.5E+30 = 4500000000000000000000000000000.

or very small numbers:

4.5E−30 = .0000000000000000000000000000045

Other examples of real numbers expressed in exponential notation are

1.9E2	= 190.0
9.8765432E3	= 9876.5432
−4.268E1	= −42.68
3.00000E−5	= 0.00003
−1.000000E−16	= −0.0000000000000001

1.23456E0	= 1.23456
6.200000E4	= 62000.0
5.17E12	= 5170000000000.0
4.56078E−1	= 0.456078
−7.90000E−2	= −0.079

In program statements, real variables may appear in decimal or exponential notation:

```
VAR
   YardSec,
   FeetSec,
   InchSec : REAL;
 . . .
   YardSec := 186000.0 * 1760.0;
   FeetSec := 1.86E5 * (1760.0 * 3.0);
   InchSec := 1.86E5 * ((1.76E3 * 3.0) * 12.0);
```

The range of real numbers may vary on different computer systems. On microcomputers, real numbers range from approximately −1.7014E38 to +1.7014E38.

The precision of real numbers is limited by the number of significant digits maintained by the computer. On 16-bit systems, seven significant digits are typically carried. Consequently, the results of real-number calculations will be only approximate in many situations. The addition calculation

```
x := 1000000.0 + 0.0000001;
```

illustrates this round-off error; when the calculation is made, the least-significant digit will be truncated, producing the value 1,000,000.

The arithmetic operators associated with variables of type REAL are

+   addition

−   subtraction

*   multiplication

/   real division

Program 2–3 illustrates the use of real variables by displaying the results of arithmetic operations using real values. The displayed results of

Program 2–3 SampleReal

```
MODULE SampleReal;      (* Demonstrate real-number arithmetic *)

FROM InOut IMPORT WriteLn;
FROM RealInOut IMPORT WriteReal;

VAR
    RaddResult,
    RsubResult,
    RmulResult,
    RdivResult : REAL;

BEGIN
    RaddResult := 25.0 + 4.0;
    RsubResult := 25.0 - 4.0;
    RmulResult := 25.0 * 4.0;
    RdivResult := 25.0 / 4.0;
    WriteLn;
    WriteReal(RaddResult, 10);
    WriteReal(RsubResult, 10);
    WriteReal(RmulResult, 10);
    WriteReal(RdivResult, 10);
    WriteLn;

END SampleReal.
```

this program are

   2.90E+01   2.10E+01   1.00E+02   6.25E+00

The procedure WriteReal, which displays the results, is the real-number counterpart of WriteInt. It is imported from the library module RealInOut, which contains procedures for input and output of real variables. WriteReal displays a real variable in a minimum field size with leading spaces. The exponent and its sign count in determining the field size. That is, "E+01" in the first displayed result occupies four positions of the ten-position field size specified in the WriteReal statement.

MathLib0

Besides using addition, subtraction, multiplication, and division, Modula-2 augments real arithmetic operations with function procedures from MathLib0, a library module. MathLib0 contains eight function procedures for performing common math calculations.

sqrt(x)	calculates square root of x (x must be positive)
exp(x)	raises e to the x power (e is the base of natural logarithms and is equal to 2.71828...)
ln(x)	calculates natural logarithm with base e (x must be > 0)
sin(x)	calculates trigonometric sine for x radians
cos(x)	calculates trigonometric cosine for x radians
arctan(x)	calculates trigonometric arctangent of x (angle in radians whose tangent is x)
real(i)	converts integer i to real value
entier(x)	converts real x to integer value

The French word for *integer* is *entier*.

(For reference, 180 degrees = *pi* radians, 360 degrees = 2 *pi* radians, 90 degrees = *pi*/2 radians, and *pi* = 3.141592654).

The trigonometric derivations of tangent, cotangent, cosecant, and secant may be obtained from the trigonometric procedures in MathLib0 through the formulas:

tangent = sin/cos
cotangent = 1/tan
cosecant = 1/sin
secant = 1/cos

Simple examples of MathLib0 procedures follow:

```
x := sqrt(49.0);        (* yields 7.0 in variable x *)
x := exp(3.0);          (* yields 20.086 in variable x *)
x := ln(20.086);        (* yields 3.0 in variable x *)
x := sin(0.5236);       (* yields 0.5 in variable x *)
x := cos(0.5236);       (* yields 0.8660 in variable x *)
x := arctan(0.5774);    (* yields 0.5236 in variable x *)
```

The procedures real and entier convert integer to real values and vice versa. In the case of entier, the fractional part of the real value is truncated. Also, if the real value cannot fit in an integer variable, the result is *unpredictable*, or *undefined*. For example,

```
x := real(93);          (* yields 9.30E+01 in variable x *)
i := entier(146.97);    (* yields 146 in variable i *)
i := entier(9.3E+30);   (* is undefined, because the real value
                           exceeds the range of integers *)
```

An application of MathLib0 procedures is shown in Program 2–4, which calculates velocity and acceleration of a swinging pendulum. The program accepts as input the pendulum length, angular velocity, and elapsed time since the pendulum passed through the bottom of its swing. It then calculates the results using standard formulas from physics.

Program 2–4 Pendulum

```
MODULE Pendulum;        (* Calculate velocity & acceleration of
                           swinging pendulum *)

FROM InOut IMPORT WriteLn,
                  WriteString;
FROM RealInOut IMPORT WriteReal,
                      ReadReal;
FROM MathLib0 IMPORT sin,
                     cos;

CONST
   fieldwidth = 10;         (* width of output field *)

VAR
   r,                       (* input—pendulum length *)
   w,                       (*        angular velocity *)
   t,                       (*        time *)
   velocity,                (* velocity result *)
   acceleration : REAL;     (* acceleration result *)
```

```
BEGIN
  WriteLn;
  WriteString("Enter pendulum length: ");
  ReadReal(r);                    (* get length from keyboard *)

  WriteLn;
  WriteString("Enter angular velocity: ");
  ReadReal(w);                    (* get velocity from keyboard *)

  WriteLn;
  WriteString("Enter time: ");
  ReadReal(t);                    (* get time from keyboard *)

  velocity := (r * w) * (cos(w * t));
  acceleration := (r * (w * w)) * (sin(w * t));

  WriteLn;
  WriteString("Velocity = ");
  WriteReal(velocity, fieldwidth);

  WriteLn;
  WriteString("Acceleration = ");
  WriteReal(acceleration, fieldwidth);

  WriteLn;

END Pendulum.
```

The program imports ReadReal, a procedure that has not yet been used in this book. ReadReal is the real counterpart of ReadInt. It reads a real value from the terminal keyboard in either decimal or exponential notation. The cardinal equivalent of ReadReal and ReadInt is ReadCard.

2.5 Mixed Arithmetic

Previously it was stated that it is illegal to mix operands of different types in arithmetic and assignment statements (with the exception that INTEGER and CARDINAL types are assignment-compatible). Situations do arise, however, in which strict typing can be overly constraining. In these cases, one type can conveniently be converted to another with standard function procedures (procedures that return values) especially designed for that purpose.

Say, for example, the average weight of people aboard a ship is being calculated. In Modula-2, a CARDINAL variable would be declared for the number of people and REAL variables would be declared for the sum of the weights and the average weight, because they entail fractional parts. These dissimilar types could then be mixed in an arithmetic calculation through the standard function FLOAT. For example,

```
VAR
    TotalWeight,
    AverageWeight : REAL;
    NumberPeople : CARDINAL;

. . .
AverageWeight := TotalWeight / (FLOAT(NumberPeople));
```

FLOAT converts a cardinal argument into a real value. FLOAT resembles the library function procedure real of module MathLib0. The two primary differences are that real converts integer instead of cardinal arguments, and real belongs to a library module that must be imported, whereas standard function procedures are integral to the languge.

The other standard function for type conversion is TRUNC. TRUNC converts a real argument into a cardinal value by truncating the fractional part. For instance, TRUNC(3.96) produces the value 3. TRUNC resembles the procedure entier in module MathLib0, except that it produces a cardinal instead of integer value.

With type-conversion functions, incompatible types can be mixed freely in arithmetic statements:

```
VAR
    r,
    x : REAL;
    c : CARDINAL;

. . .
    x := (r / FLOAT(c));
```

To conclude, the operations of FLOAT and TRUNC can be summarized as:

```
    x := FLOAT(c);    (* converts cardinal value in c to real and assigns
                         it to real variable x *)

    c := TRUNC(x);    (* converts real value in x to cardinal by truncating
                         the fractional part and assigns it to cardinal
                         variable c *)
```

2.6 Summary/Problems

Modula-2 mandates type attributes on constant and variable data items. The type attribute restricts the use of a variable to operations that are type-compatible. For constants, the type is implicit in the declaration. For variables, the type must be explicitly stated when the variable is declared in the VAR section. One exception to the type-compatibility rule is that type INTEGER is assignment-compatible with type CARDINAL.

The standard function procedures MIN and MAX furnish the lower and upper values of the types INTEGER, CARDINAL, and REAL.

Problems

1. [L] Based on the given type declarations, which of the following expressions are valid?

    ```
    VAR
        a : INTEGER;
        b : CARDINAL;
        c : REAL;
    . . .
        a := 41.3;
        b := +9;
        c := −15.88;
        b := b * c;
        c := c / 3.0;
    ```

2. [L] What value does the following expression yield? Of what type is the overall expression?

    (TRUNC(23.96) * 2) MOD TRUNC(5.1)

3. [M] The Pacific, Atlantic, and Arctic oceans are 2290, 2043 and 727 fathoms deep on the average. Write a program to convert the fathoms to feet.

4. [D] Write a program using REAL numbers to:

    a. Calculate 1.0/3.0.
    b. Multiply the calculation in step (a) by 3.0 and then subtract 1.0.
    c. Display the end result using WriteReal in a 15-character field width.

    Is the result equal to zero? Why not? Try the same calculation on a hand-held calculator. Do the results differ?

5. [M] Write a program to perform the following calculations and display the results including the fractional parts.

   a. How many fathoms are in 79,413 inches?

   b. How many meters are in a mile?

   c. The speed of sound is 1088 feet per second. What is it in miles per second?

6. [D] Write a program that calculates the area of a triangle using the formula

$$a = [s * (s-a) * (s-b) * (s-c)]^{1/2}$$

where

   a, b, and c are the lengths of the sides, and

   $s = (a+b+c)/2$

3

Principles of Navigation

3. Principles of Navigation

The programs in the first two chapters were short and simple. Like canoes and kayaks, such programs can float on the water, but their value for heavy-duty shipping is limited. This chapter enlarges those Modula-2 vessels, using constructs that propel them beyond the calm waters of the bay to the open sea of real computing.

Methods for controlling execution flow, which will be discussed first, allow programmers to chart alternate courses after the journey has begun. After that, Modula-2's ARRAY construct, which packages much of the cargo, or data, carried on ocean voyages, will be covered.

HOW CAN THE MACHINE PERFORM ITS TRICKS?

The general answer lies in the fact that computers can follow conditional instructions. They can take two values and compare them—that comes down to simple arithmetic—and, if so commanded, can perform one action if the values are equal and another if they are not. In this ability to follow conditional instructions—an ability built into the machine—lies much of the computer's power. You can set before it, in sequence, bifurcating webs of conditional instructions, until the machine appears to make sophisticated decisions on its own.

—Tracy Kidder, *The Soul of a New Machine*, 1981.

3.1 Controlling Execution Flow

An essential ingredient in a programming language is the capability to alter the path of program execution from the straight sequential flow of instructions. Alternate paths allow the program to react to different circumstances. Suppose that you're writing a program to monitor a ship's fuel. The program must determine if the fuel tank has dropped below a certain level, say 100 gallons, and display a warning message if it has. In Modula-2, this test could be written as

```
IF (FuelTank < 100) THEN
    WriteString("Warning: Fuel Low");
END;
```

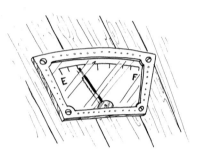

The less-than sign, <, is a *relational operator.* Relational operators, which are sometimes referred to as comparison operators, include

<	less than
>	greater than
<=	less than or equal to
>=	greater than or equal to
=	equals
# or <>	not equal to

The last relational operator, "not equal," can be written as # or <>. FuelTank # 100 has the same meaning as FuelTank <> 100.

The result of a relational operator is a binary, or *boolean,* value. These values appear so often in computer logic that Modula-2 delegates a special type called BOOLEAN to represent them. Boolean expressions and variables have one of two values, TRUE or FALSE. TRUE and FALSE are *standard identifiers* that indicate the presence or absence of a given property. They can be used to represent any dual condition, such as on/off, yes/no, male/female, or zero/one.

The following statements show the boolean results of two relational statements.

```
3 < 4       yields TRUE
14 <= -22   yields FALSE
```

In the fuel-tank test, the expression of whether or not the fuel tank was low could have been assigned to a variable of type BOO-LEAN by writing

```
VAR
    FuelTank : CARDINAL;
    TankLow : BOOLEAN;

. . .
    TankLow := (FuelTank < 100);
    IF TankLow THEN
        WriteString("Warning: Fuel Low");
    END;
```

In the assignment statement, the boolean variable TankLow assumes a TRUE or FALSE value depending on the outcome of the comparison (FuelTank < 100).

The expression IF TankLow is equivalent to saying IF TankLow = TRUE. Similarly, the expression IF NOT TankLow equates to IF TankLow = FALSE. It is considered poor style to write the expanded condition completely. As the abbreviation "e.g." (*exempli gratia*) is used in English in place of "for example," the abbreviations p for p = TRUE and NOT p for p = FALSE are used in Modula-2.

Boolean Operators

As integer variables and expressions can be combined with arithmetic operators, boolean variables and expressions can be combined with *boolean operators*. The boolean operators are: OR, AND (denoted also by &), and NOT (denoted also by ~).

If the expressions

```
VAR
    WeatherBad,
    CrewHappy : BOOLEAN;
```

are declared, the following expressions will have boolean values:

```
(FuelTank < 100) AND WeatherBad
(NOT WeatherBad) OR CrewHappy
```

Parentheses spell out explicitly the order of evaluation of boolean operators, as they do with arithmetic operators, and they should be used wherever multiple operators appear.

When boolean expressions are being constructed, a *truth table* often clarifies the possibilities. A truth table simply lists all evaluations of a boolean expression. Table 3–1 is a truth table that summarizes the three boolean expressions NOT p, p AND q, and p OR q for all possible values of p and q. This truth table shows that the expression TankLow OR WeatherBad would be false only if both TankLow and WeatherBad had FALSE values.

Table 3—1 A Truth Table Summarizing the Boolean Expressions NOT p, p AND q, and p OR q

p	q	NOT p	p AND q	p OR q
TRUE	TRUE	FALSE	TRUE	TRUE
TRUE	FALSE	FALSE	FALSE	TRUE
FALSE	TRUE	TRUE	FALSE	TRUE
FALSE	FALSE	TRUE	FALSE	FALSE

In some cases, the first part of an expression can determine the overall value of the expression, eliminating the need to examine the second part. For example, the expression p AND q will be true only if p is true. Hence, if p is false the second part of the expression can be ignored, because the entire expression will be false regardless of the value of q. Modula-2 takes advantage of this shortcut when evaluating boolean expressions.

Because such *short circuiting* of an expression is possible, the order of the operands is important, and the result may be valid even if the second operand is undefined. The latter fact means that the following type of statement may be written:

```
IF ((NumPeople # Ø) AND ((TotalWeight/NumPeople) > 15Ø))
   THEN WriteString("Average weight exceeds 15Ø");
END;
```

If NumPeople is zero, the second part of the expression will be undefined, because division by zero is illegal. The first part of the expression,

however, traps this condition when it is true and short circuits the statement.

Whenever possible, compound boolean expressions should be written to take advantage of Modula-2's short circuiting scheme. In other words, the conditions most likely to be true (in the case of OR) or false (in the case of AND) should be written first. For example,

```
VAR
   FuelTank : CARDINAL;
   HurricanePredicted : BOOLEAN;

. . .

   IF ((FuelTank < 100OR (HurricanePredicted)) THEN
      WriteString ("Set course for harbor");
   END;
```

One question that frequently arises when writing boolean expressions is whether or not mathematical-style expressions are valid. In other words, to determine if × is between 16 and 32, can the expression

```
IF (16 < × < 32)
```

be used? Likewise, can the following expression be used to determine if × is either 1, 2, or 3?

```
IF (× = 1 OR 2 OR 3)
```

The answer is no. In Modula-2, these expressions must be written as

```
IF ((16 < ×) AND (× < 32))
```

and

```
IF ((× = 1) OR (× = 2) OR (× = 3))
```

Sometimes it pays to simplify boolean expression through *transformation rules*. Two of the most useful transformations are De Morgan's laws, which state

```
(NOT p) AND (NOT q) = NOT (p OR q)
(NOT p) OR (NOT q) = NOT (p AND q)
```

These equations simplify an expression with three boolean operators to an equivalent expression with only two boolean operators.

GREATEST DISCOVERY OF THE NINETEENTH CENTURY

Born into an impecunious lower-class tradesman's family at Lincoln, England, George Boole [1815–1864] had only a common school education. He learned both Greek and Latin independently, believing that this knowledge would help him to rise above his station. During his early years as an elementary school teacher, Boole found that he had to learn more mathematics, and he began mastering the works of Laplace and Lagrange, as well as studying additional foreign languages. Having become friendly with Augustus De Morgan, he also took a keen interest in a controversy over logic that the Scottish philosopher Sir William Hamilton had raised with De Morgan. The result was that Boole in 1847 published a short work entitled *The Mathematical Analysis of Logic,* a little book that De Morgan recognized as epoch-making.

A great mathematician and philosopher of the twentieth century, Bertrand Russell, has asserted that the greatest discovery of the nineteenth century was the nature of pure mathematics. He adds to this claim the words, "Pure Mathematics was discovered by Boole."

—Carl B. Boyer, *A History of Mathematics,* 1968.

3.2 IF

All this detail about boolean expressions may seem out of place in a section on execution flow, but describing the conditional statements that control execution without having first established a foundation in boolean expressions is putting the cart before the horse.

With the cart and the horse where they should be, it is possible to begin examining the hows and whys of execution flow, starting with the general form of the conditional statement, IF:

```
IF condition-1 THEN statement-sequence-1
ELSIF condition-2 THEN statement-sequence-2
ELSIF condition-3 THEN statement-sequence-3
. . .
ELSIF condition-n-1 THEN statement-sequence-n-1
ELSE statement-sequence
END;
```

Condition-1 through condition-n-1 are *boolean expressions* that are evaluated sequentially. When the first true condition is reached, the corresponding statement or statements (represented by statement-sequence-1 through n-1) are executed and the remainder of the IF statement, if any, is ignored. If none of the conditions is satisfied, the statement(s) following the ELSE clause is executed. In Modula-2, ELSE conveys the same meaning as the word *otherwise* does in English. If only one condition is being tested with a single course of action, the optional ELSIF and ELSE clauses may be omitted. The fuel-monitoring example shown earlier demonstrates this. It tests only one condition, namely, if the fuel tank is low:

```
IF (FuelTank < 100) THEN
   WriteString("Warning: Fuel Low");
END;
```

In a more complicated situation, this example could be expanded to check a reserve tank if the regular tank is low.

```
IF (FuelTank >= 100) THEN
   WriteString("Fuel Adequate:);
ELSIF (ReserveTank >= 100) THEN
   WriteString("Warning: Fuel Low But Reserve Adequate");
ELSE
   WriteString("Warning: Fuel Desperately Low");
END;
```

To express an either/or situation, the IF statement can be written without the ELSIF clause. That is,

```
IF (FuelTank >= 100) THEN
   WriteString("Fuel Adequate");
ELSE
   WriteString("Should Refill Main Tank");
END;
```

The statements following the THEN and ELSE clauses can be multiple statements, too.

```
IF (FuelTank < 100) THEN
   WriteString("Warning: Fuel Low");
   TankLow := TRUE;
END;
```

Additionally, the statements following THEN and ELSE clauses may be other IF statements. An IF statement containing embedded IF statements is called a *nested* IF. For example,

```
IF (FuelTank < 100) THEN
   IF (WeatherBad) THEN
      Writestring("Warning: Advise Return to Port");
   ELSE
      WriteString("Continue but Conserve Fuel");
   END;
ELSE      (* fuel okay *)
   WriteString("Fuel Adequate");
END;
```

This program segment also demonstrates use of Modula-2's free format to spatially group statements that are logically connected. For example, the previous instructions could have been written as

```
IF (FuelTank < 100) THEN IF (WeatherBad) THEN
WriteString("Warning: Return to Port"); ELSE
WriteString("Continue but Conserve Fuel"); END; ELSE
(* fuel okay *)WriteString("Fuel Adequate"); END;
```

Trying to understand this hodgepodge overheats the optic nerve. It's not clear where statements start and end. Obviously, the program is easier to read and understand when it is indented and aligned, a practical rule known as *prettyprinting*.

PRETTYPRINTING

Prettyprinting refers to the spacing of programs to illuminate their logical structure. Programs that conform to the tenets of prettyprinting align statements that are logically grouped together and indent local statements that are part of larger logical units. Parallel sections of code are indented to the same margin. Inner blocks of code, such as the bodies of loops, procedures, and IF statements, are indented even farther. Spaces and blank lines serve to delineate functional segments.

The spatial formatting aids debugging and program maintenance immensely. It is fairly easy to detect errors such as misplaced sections and improperly nested blocks. A programmer trying to read and follow the program's logic does not have to consciously devote time to unravelling the structure.

Prettyprinting adds indisputable clarity to programs. If your program has polished structure, show it!

Program 3–1, which calculates the average weight of a group of people, shows how the IF statement controls execution. The program accepts as input the number of people in the group and the total weight.

Program 3–1 CalcWeight

```
MODULE CalcWeight;        (* Calculate average weight *)

FROM InOut IMPORT WriteString,
                  WriteLn,
                  ReadCard;

FROM RealInOut IMPORT ReadReal,
                      WriteReal;

VAR
   NumPeople : CARDINAL;
   TotalWeight,
   AverageWeight : REAL;

BEGIN
   WriteString("Enter number of people: ");
   ReadCard(NumPeople);      (* get group size from keyboard *)

   IF (NumPeople # 0) THEN        (* avoid division by 0 *)
      WriteLn;
      WriteString("Total Weight? ");
      ReadReal(TotalWeight);
      AverageWeight := TotalWeight / FLOAT(NumPeople);
      WriteLn;
      WriteString("Average weight is ");
      WriteReal(AverageWeight, 10);
      WriteLn;
   ELSE
      WriteString("Number must be > 0 to calculate average");
   END;

END CalcWeight.
```

Because division by zero is impossible, the program checks to see if the number entered for calculating the average is zero. If it is, the program simply displays a message to that effect and terminates. Otherwise, the program calculates the average weight and displays it. Notice that the calculation is performed using the standard procedure FLOAT, which converts the cardinal variable, NumPeople, to a real value.

3.3 CASE

The IF statement selects alternative courses of action based on the evaluation of a list of conditions. Another way of selecting alternatives is through the CASE statement. The CASE statement produces the same net effect of a certain class of IF statements, but in a more elegant manner. For example, the following statements show one way of converting the numeric symbols for the first three months of the year to strings (remember, a *string* is any sequence of characters enclosed in double quotation marks):

```
VAR
   mm : CARDINAL;
 . . .
   IF (mm = 1) THEN
      WriteString("Jan.");
   ELSIF (mm = 2) THEN
      WriteString("Feb.");
   ELSIF (mm = 3) THEN
      WriteString("Mar.");
   ELSE
      WriteString("Not Jan., Feb. or Mar.");
   END;
```

If CASE were used instead of IF, this expression would be

```
CASE mm of
   1 : WriteString("Jan."); |
   2 : WriteString("Feb."); |
   3 : WriteString("Mar.");
ELSE
   WriteString("Not Jan., Feb. or Mar.");
END;
```

The vertical bar, |, separates the statements for each case. It is not needed after the last case preceding the ELSE clause.

The general form of the CASE statement is

```
CASE expression OF
   case-1 : statement-sequence-1; |
   case-2 : statement-sequence-2; |
   case-3 : statement-sequence-3; |
    . . .
   case-n : statement-sequence-n;
ELSE
   statement-sequence;
END;
```

Case-1 through case-n represent *case labels.* These must be constants or constant expressions. They may appear individually or in a list. As with the IF statement, the statement sequences following each case may be single statements or groups of statements. For example, a program segment to determine the number of days in a given month could be written as

```
VAR
   yy,                          (* two-digit year *)
   mm,                          (* two-digit month *)
   len : CARDINAL;              (* length in days *)

 . . .
   CASE mm OF
      1, 3, 5, 7, 8, 10, 12 :   (* must be Jan, Mar, May, *)
         len := 31; |           (* Jul, Aug, Oct or Dec *)
      4, 6, 9, 11 :             (* must be Apr, Jun, Sep *)
         len := 30; |           (* or Nov *)
      2 :                       (* must be Feb, check leap yr *)
         IF (((yy MOD 4) = 0) AND ((yy MOD 100) # 0)) THEN
            len := 29;          (* if year is divisible by 4 *)
         ELSE                   (* and it is not divisible by *)
            len := 28;          (* 100, then year is leap *)
         END; (* IF *)          (* and Feb. has 29 days *)
   ELSE
      WriteString("Invalid month");
   END;      (* CASE *)
```

The third case label, the case of the month equalling 2, for February, contains logic to check for a leap year.

The preceding program segment contains two ENDs. The comment immediately following the END indicates which statement, the IF or the CASE, is being terminated. This comment is optional and appears merely for the benefit of the human reader.

CASE statements may also be used with boolean constant values. For example, you can write

```
CASE TankLow OF
  TRUE : WriteString("Warning: Fuel Low"); |
  FALSE : WriteString("Fuel Adequate");
END;
```

Notice that this example omits the ELSE clause. With the CASE statement, as with the IF statement, the ELSE part is optional. If the CASE contains no ELSE part and none of the CASE labels matches the CASE expression, an execution error occurs.

The statement sequence following a CASE label may be null to allow for a "no-operation" condition. For example, after the sequence

```
mm := 2;
len := 28;
CASE mm OF
  1, 3, 5, 7, 8, 10, 12 :
    len := 31; |
  2 : ; |          (* do nothing if case variable equals 2 *)
  4, 6, 9, 11 :
    len := 30;
END;
```

the variable len will still equal 28.

The main difference between CASE and IF statement is that the conditions in an IF statement are boolean expressions, whereas the labels in a CASE statement are constants. A CASE statement of the form

```
CASE (FuelTank − 100) OF
  < 0: WriteString("Warning: Fuel Low"); |
  > 0: WriteString("Fuel Adequate");
END;
```

is *illegal* because the CASE labels are not constants.

Overall, the CASE statement allows you to quickly identify the different conditions and their corresponding instruction sequences. It offers the advantage of being less wordy and more readable than the IF statement, but lacks flexibility, because CASE labels cannot be boolean expressions.

3.4 Looping

So far, all of the programs presented have executed sequentially. Alternate paths of execution have been selected using IF and CASE statements, but the flow has still been from top to bottom. Although this type of execution is useful in many applications, much of the power of a computer stems from its capability to repeat tasks over and over. Modula-2 exploits this capability by offering a rich assortment of instructions for *looping*, or performing repetitive execution.

REPEAT

The first instruction for looping is called, appropriately, REPEAT. Its general form is

```
REPEAT
    statement sequence
UNTIL expression;
```

For example, the following program segment calculates two raised to the nth power, where n is positive.

```
VAR
    power : CARDINAL;
    answer : REAL;
. . .
    ReadCard(power);          (* get exponent from keyboard *)
    answer := 1.0;            (* initialize answer *)
    IF (power # 0) THEN       (* power # 0? *)
        REPEAT                (* yes—do loop *)
            answer := answer * 2.0;
            DEC(power);
        UNTIL (power = 0);
    END; (* IF *)
    WriteReal(answer, 12);    (* show result *)
```

The instructions between the REPEAT and UNTIL statements are termed the *loop body* and are executed repetitively until the exit condition is satisfied. The exit condition, (power = 0), is tested after each execution of the loop body.

In addition to the REPEAT instruction, this program segment introduces the standard procedure DEC, which decrements a variable by 1. Related to DEC are procedures for decrementing by a value and incrementing. Together they consist of

DEC($\times$) performs the operation $\times := \times - 1$
DEC($\times$,n) performs the operation $\times := \times - n$
INC($\times$) performs the operation $\times := \times + 1$
INC($\times$,n) performs the operation $\times := \times + n$

The symbol n represents any expression compatible with $\times$, including variables. DEC and INC accept variables of types INTEGER and CARDINAL but not REAL.

Because the termination condition of a REPEAT loop is not evaluated until the end of the loop, the body of the loop will always be executed at least once. For example, the program segment

```
i := 0;
j := 0;
REPEAT
  INC(j);
UNTIL (i = 0);
WriteInt(j,6);
```

displays one as the value of j.

When working with REPEAT loops, keep in mind the two main operational characteristics:

1. The body of the loop will be executed at least once before the termination condition is evaluated.

2. The termination condition must be satisfied eventually or you've created the Bermuda Triangle of programming, the infinite loop.

WHILE

REPEAT loops come in handy, but you don't always want to have to drive around the block once before deciding you'd rather not take the ride. For these situations, the WHILE loop is ideal. It tests the exit condition before the loop is executed.

The process of raising 2 to the *n*th power can be expressed with a WHILE loop as

```
ReadReal(power);      (* get exponent from keyboard *)
answer := 1.0;        (* initialize answer *)
```

```
WHILE (power # 0) DO
   answer := answer * 2.0;
   DEC(power);  power :=
END;      (* WHILE *)
WriteReal(answer,12);      (* show result *)
```

If the initial value of power is 0, the loop will not execute even one time (but the answer will still be correct, because 2 to the 0 power equals one).

Overall, the WHILE statement is used more often than the REPEAT statement, because it allows the possibility that the loop may not be executed at all.

FOR

In situations in which a statement sequence is executed repeatedly with a progression of values, the FOR statement expresses the problem succinctly. For example, raising 2 to a power can be written in yet another flavor as

```
answer := 1.0;
FOR i := power TO 1 BY −1 DO
   answer := answer * 2.0;
END;
```

This sequence causes repetitive execution of the statements in the loop body, that is, the statements between DO and END. The loop is repeated for the values i = power, i = power-1, i = power-2, ... i = 1.

The FOR statement takes the general form

```
FOR control-variable := expression-1 TO expression-2 BY
                        constant-expression DO
   statement sequence;
END;
```

Expression-1 specifies the starting value; expression-2, the limit; and constant-expression, the increment or decrement. The constant-expression must be of type INTEGER or CARDINAL. A positive value signifies an increment; a negative value, a decrement. If the constant-expression is not specified, it is assumed to be an increment of value 1.

If the control-variable is numeric, it must be of type CARDINAL or INTEGER. Furthermore, the types of expression-1 and expression-2 must be compatible with it. REAL variables are illegal.

If the constant-expression is an increment and expression-1 is greater than expression-2, the statement sequence will not be executed at all. Similarly, if the constant-expression is a decrement and expression-1 is less than expression-2, the statement sequence will not be executed.

For example, in

```
j := 5
FOR i := 8 TO j BY 1 DO
   statement sequence
END;
```

the statement sequence will be bypassed completely.

Two implicit rules govern the use of FOR loops:

1. The statement sequence should not change the value of the control-variable; otherwise, the results may be unpredictable.

2. When the loop terminates, no assumption can be made about the value of the control-variable, although we know that the terminating condition was met. The actual value of the control-variable at termination should be regarded as *undefined*.

In general, a FOR statement can be expressed by an equivalent WHILE statement. The following two statements produce the same effect.

```
FOR i := 1 TO 99 BY 2 DO
   statement sequence;
END;
```

```
i := 1;
WHILE(i <= 99) DO
   statement sequence;
   INC(i,2);
END;
```

The FOR statement is not exactly equivalent to the WHILE statement, because when the WHILE statement terminates, it has been established that $i = 99$, whereas the FOR control-variable is undefined.

Although the FOR and WHILE statements seem nearly identical, there are two reasons for choosing FOR over WHILE wherever possible. First, the FOR statement imparts more information to the human reader. The range of the control variable and the number of times the loop will be executed are both immediately apparent. Second, the compiler can take advantage of this same information to generate a more efficient program from a FOR statement than from an equivalent WHILE statement.

LOOP

The final repetitive construct is called simply LOOP. LOOP is distinguished from the other repetitive instructions in that the terminating condition, if any, may be placed anywhere in the body of the loop. This flexibility comes in handy for addressing two programming situations.

First, you can write the infamous infinite loop. Infinite loops contradict what is taught in Programming 101, but there are still situations in which they alone can fill the bill. For example, in multiprogramming (the concurrent execution of multiple progams), a control program might invoke a monitor program to constantly sense a certain condition—say, to read a thermometer and display the current temperature. The initiation and termination of this monitor program are handled by the control program. Because the monitor program has no internal termination condition, a LOOP sequence without an exit would precisely suit its activity.

Another application of LOOP arises when we want to exit from the middle of a loop body. For example, to calculate powers of 2 until a 0 power is entered, these statements could be used:

```
WriteString("Calculating powers of two");
WriteLn;
WriteString("Enter number or zero to terminate");
LOOP
    answer := 1.0;
    ReadReal(power);              (* get exponent from keyboard *)
    IF (power = 0) THEN           (* zero? *)
        EXIT;                     (* yes—quit and leave loop *)
    END;    (* IF *)
    WHILE (power # 0) DO          (* no—calculate power of 2 *)
        answer := answer * 2.0;
        power := DEC(power);
    END;       (* WHILE *)
    WriteReal(answer,12);         (* show result *)
END;      (* LOOP *)             (* do another *)
WriteLn;
WriteString("Program terminated by operator");
```

This program segment terminates when a 0 value is entered as the power or exponent. EXIT transfers control to the instruction following the END statement of the LOOP.

Placing the EXIT at the end or beginning of the loop achieves the same result as a REPEAT, WHILE, or FOR statement. LOOP statements should be reserved, however, for situations requiring their unique capabilities. The exit conditions of REPEAT, WHILE, and FOR statements are easier identified than LOOP. Using LOOP in place of REPEAT, WHILE, or FOR accomplishes nothing; moreover, it obscures a clearer expression of the problem.

3.5 Character Data

Four different types of variables have been covered so far: INTEGER, CARDINAL, REAL, and BOOLEAN. All of these except the last express numeric data. Numbers and boolean data, however, constitute only part of the data that computers work with. The other part is characters. How does Modula-2 handle the letters of the alphabet, punctuation symbols, and other non-numeric characters? The answer lies with type CHAR.

Constants of type CHAR, like strings, are denoted with double or single quotation marks. For example,

```
VAR
    reply : CHAR;
. . .
    reply := "Y";
```

assigns the character Y to the variable REPLY. Other character representations are

","	represents comma
"t"	represents *t*
" "	represents space
"'"	represents single quotation mark

CHAR, like types INTEGER, CARDINAL, and REAL, has its own read and write routines. These are called Read and Write, without suffixes, and are imported from module InOut. The following program segment demonstrates the use of Read:

```
VAR
    reply : CHAR;
. . .
    REPEAT                        (* ask question until reply is valid *)
        WriteString("Do you wish to continue? ")
        Read(reply);
```

```
UNTIL ((reply  =  "Y")  OR        (* check upper-case and *)
        (reply  =  "y")  OR        (* lower-case valid *)
        (reply  =  "N")  OR        (* answers *)
        (reply  =  "n"));
```

CHAR values may be any of the 128 characters defined by the ASCII character table, which is listed in Appendix C. Each character in the table corresponds with an *ordinal number* in the range 0 through 127. The ordinal number simply indicates the rank or relative position within the table. Ordinal numbers are used for conversions and comparisons of CHAR data.

Comparisons of CHAR values, like those of INTEGER and REAL, are made with *relational operators.* According to the ASCII table,

"A" < "B" < "C" < ... < "Z"

and

"0" < "1" < "2" < ... < "9"

Relational operators, incidentally, are the only operators besides the assignment operator that may be used with type CHAR.

Of the 128 characters in the table, 95 are displayable and printable. The other 33, with ordinal numbers 0 through 32, are reserved for control functions, such as carriage return, line feed, and so on. If a character is nondisplayable, how can it be entered as data in a program? Modula-2 provides the standard functions CHR and ORD to convert ordinal numbers to characters and vice versa.

As an example, consider the character "Y." In the ASCII table, it appears as ordinal value 89. Thus, the expression

ORD("Y")

yields 89.

The ordinal numbers generated by the ORD function are of type CARDINAL, and they range from 0 to 127.

To convert the ordinal number back to a character, the inverse of the ORD function, CHR, is used. Specifically,

CHR(89)

yields "Y."

Because these functions are inverses of each other, the expression

ORD(CHR(89))

yields 89.

Keep in mind when working with these functions that ORD("0") is equal to 48, not 0.

One standard function that operates only on variables of type CHAR is CAP. CAP performs capitalization, that is, it returns the upper-case equivalent of a lower-case character. If the character is already upper-case or if it is nonalphabetic, it is returned unchanged. Some examples follow:

CAP("n")	yields "N"
CAP("N")	yields "N"
CAP("2")	yields "2"
CAP("%")	yields "%"

This function allows the test for a yes or no reply written earlier as

```
REPEAT                          (* ask question until reply is valid *)
    WriteString("Do you wish to continue? ");
    Read(reply);
UNTIL ((reply = "Y") OR         (* check upper-case and *)
       (reply = "y") OR         (* lower-case answers *)
       (reply = "N") OR
       (reply = "n"));
```

to be shortened to the form

```
REPEAT                             (* ask question until reply is valid *)
    WriteString("Do you wish to continue? ");
    Read(reply);
UNTIL ((CAP(reply) = "Y") OR    (* check upper-case and *)
(CAP(reply) = "N"));            (* lower-case answers *)
```

The standard procedures for incrementing and decrementing also operate on type CHAR. Some examples follow:

INC("A")	yields "B"
INC("A",3)	yields "D"
DEC(CHR(89))	yields "X"
DEC(ORD("Y"),2)	yields 87

Program 3–2 uses data of type CHAR and associated operations to convert a sequence of upper-case hexadecimal (base 16) characters to a cardinal value and then display the result. The program reads the hexadecimal sequence character by character. A space indicates the end of the characters. The precise algorithm is:

1. Set variable DecEquiv to 0. This variable will hold the decimal equivalent of the hexadecimal string.

2. Read a character from the keyboard.

3. Echo the character on the terminal screen.

4. Is this character a space? If yes, quit. Otherwise, assume that it's a hexadecimal character.

5. Multiply DecEquiv by 16.

6. If the character is "0" . . . "9", then add 0 . . . 9 to DecEquiv; otherwise, assume that the character is "A" . . . "F" and add 10 . . . 15 to DecEquiv.

7. Go to step 2.

Program 3–2 ConvertHex

```
MODULE ConvertHex;       (* Convert hex string to decimal value *)

FROM InOut IMPORT WriteLn,
                  Write,
                  Read,
                  WriteCard;

VAR
   ch : CHAR;
   DecEquiv : CARDINAL;

BEGIN
   DecEquiv := 0;                (* initialize decimal equivalent *)

   LOOP
      Read(ch);                  (* get a character *)
      Write(ch);                 (* echo character *)
      IF (ch = " ") THEN         (* end of entry? *)
         EXIT;                   (* yes *)
      END;     (* IF *)
      DecEquiv := DecEquiv * 16;
      IF (ch <= "9") THEN        (* character between 0–9?*)
         DecEquiv := DecEquiv + (ORD(ch) – ORD("0"));
      ELSE
         DecEquiv := DecEquiv + (ORD(ch) – ORD("A")) + 10;
      END;      (* IF *)
   END;      (* LOOP *)

   WriteLn;
   WriteCard(DecEquiv,5);        (* display converted result *)
   WriteLn;

END ConvertHex.
```

After each character is entered, the program "echoes" or displays it on the screen so that the operator can see what is being typed. Read is the only procedure in InOut that does not automatically echo characters on the screen. Procedures ReadCard, ReadInt, and ReadString do echo. The keyboard entry logic is simply a plain implementation—invalid characters are not screened, nor are backspaces processed.

3.6 Arrays

The types discussed up to this point, INTEGER, CARDINAL, REAL, BOOLEAN, and CHAR, all denote single values. These single-value types are referred to as *unstructured* types. The *structured* type ARRAY allows multiple values to be stored under one variable name.

The distinction between unstructured variables and arrays resembles the difference between the duties of a small tugboat's mail steward and those of a mail steward on a 2000-passenger ocean liner. On the tugboat, the steward knows the crew members personally and organizes the mail by individual names. The liner steward, on the other hand, must deal with thousands of patrons, who, for all practical purposes, are identical. The cabin location is the key to differentiating these "identical" patrons.

A similar situation arises in programming. When dealing with small quantities of data or variables, the programmer can label each one and still

keep track of them. With large numbers of variables, the programmer often must group the data items and refer to them through arrays. Each element of the array has a unique location.

Arrays are commonly used for storing tables of information: for example, the age of each crew member of a ship; the depths of the harbors in Spain; or the average windspeeds in the Gulf of Mexico for each month of the year. Arrays also come into play when strings of characters are being processed. The string "Sitting on the dock of the bay" is considered to be an array of 30 characters.

Program 3–3 uses an array to calculate the average age of the crew of a ship with 25 members. The array in this program, CrewAge, is declared

Program 3–3 AverageAge

```
MODULE AverageAge;      (* Calculate average age *)

FROM InOut IMPORT WriteLn,
                  WriteString,
                  ReadCard;
FROM RealInOut IMPORT WriteReal;

VAR
  i : CARDINAL;
  average : REAL;
  CrewAge : ARRAY[1..25] OF CARDINAL;

BEGIN
  WriteLn;
  WriteString("Enter crew ages: ");
  WriteLn;

  FOR i := 1 TO 25 BY 1 DO
    ReadCard(CrewAge[i]);      (* get age from keyboard *)
    WriteLn;
  END;

  average := 0.0;
  FOR i := 1 TO 25 BY 1 DO      (* sum ages *)
    average := average + FLOAT(CrewAge[i]);
  END;

  average := average / 25.0;      (* calculate average *)
  WriteLn;
  WriteString("Average age = ");
  WriteReal(average, 10);
  WriteLn;

END AverageAge.
```

in the VAR section. It contains 25 *elements* of type CARDINAL, which are accessed individually through the *array index* by writing CrewAge[i]. The type rules for CARDINAL apply to each element.

The array index ranges from 1 to 25. In general, the index range of an array is expressed as constant-expression-1 . . constant-expression-2, bounded by brackets. For example,

```
StatePopulations : ARRAY [1..50] OF REAL:
WeekRainfall : ARRAY [1..7] OF REAL;
SurfaceTemperatures : ARRAY [-10..+10] OF INTEGER;
```

StatePopulations could represent the population figures for each of the fifty states in the United States; WeekRainfall, the rainfall in inches for each day of the week; SurfaceTemperatures, the temperatures at distances ranging from 10 feet below to 10 feet above the surface of the water.

The next program, Program 3–4, provides an example of manipulating the data within an array; this program sorts the ages of the crew members by using a bubble-sort algorithm.

Program 3–4 sorts the CrewAge array in ascending numerical sequence (smallest value first). The boolean variable sorted indicates the sort status of the array. Initially, it is set true. If the entire array can be passed through without making exchanges, then it remains true, indicating that the sort is complete.

Program 3–4 SortAge

```
MODULE SortAge;      (* Sort ages *)

FROM InOut IMPORT WriteLn,
                  WriteString,
                  WriteCard,
                  ReadCard;

VAR
   i,                              (* array index *)
   HoldAge : CARDINAL;
   sorted : BOOLEAN;
   CrewAge : ARRAY[1..25] OF CARDINAL;

BEGIN
   WriteLn;
   WriteString("Enter crew ages: ");
   WriteLn;

   FOR i := 1 TO 25 BY 1 DO
      ReadCard(CrewAge[i]);        (* get age from keyboard *)
      WriteLn;
```

```
END;
   REPEAT                           (* pass thru array until
                                        sorted *)
      sorted := TRUE;               (* assume sorted *)
      FOR i := 1 TO (25 - 1) BY 1 DO
         (* compare each adjacent pair of elements *)
         IF (CrewAge[i] > CrewAge[i+1]) THEN
            HoldAge := CrewAge[i];    (* out of order, exchange *)
            CrewAge[i] := CrewAge[i+1];
            CrewAge[i+1] := HoldAge;
            sorted := FALSE;
         END;      (* IF *)
      END;       (* FOR *)
   UNTIL sorted;

   WriteString("Sorted crew ages: ");
   FOR i := 1 TO 25 BY 1 DO          (* display sorted ages *)
      WriteCard(CrewAge[i],5);
      WriteLn;
   END;       (* FOR *)

END SortAge.
```

Array Assignment

In the previous examples, we accessed the array through its individual elements, but arrays can also be accessed as units. For example, one way of copying array a to array b is copying it element by element, namely,

```
VAR
   a : ARRAY[0..99] OF CHAR;
   b : ARRAY[0..99] OF CHAR;
   i : CARDINAL;
. . .
   FOR i := 0 TO 99 BY 1 DO
      b[i] := a[i];
   END;
```

but it's simpler to write

```
   b := a;
```

which has the same effect, because the *assignment operator* applies to entire arrays, too.

When copying an entire array with the assignment operator, you must ensure that the *sizes*, *types*, and *index ranges* of both arrays match. The following two arrays are considered assignment-compatible:

```
CrewAge : ARRAY[1..25] OF CARDINAL;
PassengerAge : ARRAY[1..25] OF CARDINAL;
```

Examples of *incompatible* arrays are

```
CrewAge : ARRAY[1..25] OF CARDINAL;
DeckhandAge : ARRAY[0..24] OF CARDINAL;
```

```
CrewAge : ARRAY[1..25] OF CARDINAL;
ShipmateAge : ARRAY[1..10] OF CARDINAL;
```

```
CrewAge : ARRAY[1..25] OF CARDINAL;
SailorAge : ARRAY[1..25] OF INTEGER;
```

```
a : ARRAY[-999..+999] OF CHAR;
b : ARRAY[-999..+999] OF REAL;
```

The first and second pairs are assignment-incompatible as entire arrays because their index ranges disagree. The third and fourth pairs are incompatible because their base types disagree. Although the first, second, and third pairs are assignment-incompatible as entire arrays, their *elements* are assignment-compatible. Thus the expressions

```
CrewAge[1] := DeckhandAge[0];
```

and

```
CrewAge[i] := SailorAge[i];
```

would be legal, even though it would be illegal to write

```
CrewAge := DeckhandAge;
```

or

```
CrewAge := SailorAge;
```

Modula-2, as was previously mentioned, regards string as arrays. Actually, it regards them as arrays of type CHAR whose indexes range from 0 to $n-1$, where n is the length of the array. Thus, the statement

```
WriteString("Aye, Aye");
```

has the same effect as

```
CONST
  response = "Aye, Aye";
  . . .
  WriteString(response);
```

or

```
VAR
  response : ARRAY[0..7] OF CHAR;
. . .
  response := "Aye, Aye";
  WriteString(response);
```

The assignment of strings to CHAR arrays follows the general rules for array assignments, with one exception. The length of the string can be equal to or *less than* the array. If the string is shorter, null characters are appended to the array to make up the difference.

A *null character* is the first character of the ASCII table. It is not displayable or printable but can be expressed as CHR(0), which means the character with the ordinal number of 0.

The following examples illustrate what happens to the response array following three different string assignments.

```
  response := "Aye, Aye";
```

After the assignment, response contains the arrangement of values shown in Figure 3–1.

"A"	"y"	"e"	","	" "	"A"	"y"	"e"

Figure 3–1

```
  response := "Aye";
```

After the assignment, response contains the values represented in Figure 3–2.

"A"	"y"	"e"	CHR(0)	CHR(0)	CHR(0)	CHR(0)	CHR(0)

Figure 3–2

```
  response := " ";
```

After the assignment, response contains the values shown in Figure 3–3.

CHR(0)	CHR(0)	CHR(0)	CHR(0)	CHR(0)	CHR(0)	CHR(0)	CHR(0)

Figure 3–3

In the last example, the two double quotation marks without embedded characters indicate a *null string*.

Although short strings can be assigned to longer arrays, as just demonstrated, the inverse does not hold true. If a long string is assigned to a shorter array, the compiler will generate an error message.

Strings of length one are treated as type CHAR. The following statements demonstrate this level of compatibility:

```
VAR
   a : ARRAY [1..1] OF CHAR;
   b,
   c : CHAR;

. . .
   a := "X";
   b := a;
   a := c;
```

The assignment operator is the only operator that applies to entire arrays. The arithmetic operators (+, −, etc.) and the relational operators (<, >, etc.) may be used on the elements of an array, but not on the entire array itself. For example, to increment each element of the CrewAge array by five, the following statements would have to be written:

```
FOR i := 1 TO 25 BY 1 DO
   CrewAge[i] := CrewAge[i] + 5;
END;
```

The statement

```
CrewAge := CrewAge + 5;
```

is *illegal*.

Similarly "zeroing out" the array would require the statements

```
FOR i := 1 TO 25 BY 1 DO
  CrewAge[i] := Ø;
END;
```

instead of

```
CrewAge := Ø;
```

which is *illegal*.

An example of an array application is given in Program 3–5, which generates prime numbers. The program calculates the 1899 prime numbers between 3 and 16,381 using the Sieve of Eratosthenes algorithm, a popular benchmark for gauging hardware and software performance. The generated primes are displayed on the terminal screen.

Program 3–5 Prime

```
MODULE Prime;       (* Generate prime numbers *)

FROM InOut IMPORT WriteLn,
                  WriteCard,
                  WriteString;

CONST
  Flg Size = 819Ø;       (* array size *)
*b
VAR
  Flags : ARRAY[Ø..Flg Size] OF BOOLEAN;
               (* indicates primes
```
if nth element = TRUE, then $n + n + 3$ is prime
if nth element = FALSE, then $n + n + 3$ is not prime
(n ranges from 0 to 8190) *)

```
  i,                         (* indexes for *)
  k,                         (* Flags array *)
  Prime,                     (* prime number *)
  Count : CARDINAL;          (* number of primes found *)

BEGIN
  Count := Ø;                         (* initialize num. found *)
  FOR i := Ø TO Flg Size BY 1 DO      (* initialize array as *)
    Flags[i] := TRUE;                 (* all prime *)
  END;
```

```
FOR i := 0 TO Flg Size BY 1 DO

    IF Flags[i] THEN                (* prime? *)
        Prime := i + i + 3;         (* yes—calculate next one *)
        WriteCard(Prime, 7);        (* display prime *)
        k := i + Prime;             (* index to multiple *)
        WHILE (k <= Flg Size) DO    (* indicate multiple nonprime *)
        Flags[k] := FALSE;
        INC(k, Prime);              (* increment to next nonprime *)
        END;                        (* WHILE *)
        INC(Count);                 (* increment primes found *)
    END;      (* IF *)

END;      (* FOR i *)               (* check next number *)

WriteLn;                            (* display result *)
WriteCard(Count, 6);
WriteString(" primes");
WriteLn;

END Prime.
```

Multidimensional Arrays

The arrays discussed so far have been *one-dimensional*. The base type of an array, however, can itself be an array. These kinds of arrays are called *multidimensional arrays* or *matrices*. For example, if there are five ships—a barge, tug, tanker, transport, and icebreaker—in each of the four oceans—the Atlantic, Pacific, Indian, and Arctic—the crew sizes of each ship could be stored in an array declared as

```
OceanShipSize : ARRAY[1..4] OF
                ARRAY[1..5] OF CARDINAL:
```

This *two-dimensional array* can be thought of as a table with four rows and five columns.

Multidimensional arrays are not limited to two dimensions. Modula-2 places no limitations on the dimensions of an array. In actual practice, the compiler or memory size of the system will effectively restrict the number of array dimensions, although the limit will probably be more than adequate.

An example of a three-dimensional array would be the crew sizes of the ships in the oceans for the summer and winter:

```
SeasonOceanShipSize : ARRAY[1..2] OF
                      ARRAY[1..4] OF
                      ARRAY[1..5] OF CARDINAL;
```

This array consists of 2 × 4 × 5, or 40, elements.

The elements of multidimensional arrays are accessed by specifying the indexes according to the order of the declaration. For example,

SeasonOceanShipSize[2,3,4]

specifies the crew size of the transport (fourth ship) in the Indian Ocean (third ocean) in the winter (second season).

The declarations of multidimensional arrays can be abbreviated to the form

SeasonOceanShipSize : ARRAY[1..2],[1..4],[1..5] OF CARDINAL;

This book will stick to the indented form, however, because it better exhibits the hierarchical structure.

In multidimensional arrays, omitting an index means that you're referring to a base array within the entire array. For example,

SeasonOceanShipSize[1,2]

refers to the crew sizes of the five ships in the Pacific (second ocean) in the summer (first season).

Similarly, you can transfer entire base arrays within arrays by following the same format. For example,

SeasonOceanShipSize[1] := SeasonOceanShipSize[2];

copies the crew sizes of all five ships and four oceans from the second season to the first season. A total of 4 × 5, or 20, elements are copied.

You might think that you could make assignments between identical base arrays within arrays having different dimensions. That is,

```
VAR
    OceanShipSize : ARRAY[1..4] OF
                          ARRAY[1..5] OF CARDINAL;
    SeasonOceanShipSize : ARRAY[1..2] OF
                                ARRAY[1..4] OF
                                    ARRAY[1..5] OF CARDINAL;
    . . .
    SeasonOceanShipSize[1,1] := OceanShipSize[1];
```

This kind of assignment is, however, illegal, because the overall dimensions of the arrays conflict.

Operations on multidimensional arrays often require multiple loops. To zero out the array SeasonOceanShipSize, these statements would be used:

```
    (* initialize first season, first ocean crew *)
FOR i := 1 TO 5 BY 1 DO
    SeasonOceanShipSize[1,1,i] := 0;
END;

    (* initialize first season, remaining oceans/crews *)
FOR i := 2 TO 4 BY 1 DO
    SeasonOceanShipSize[1,i] := SeasonOceanShipSize[1,1];
END;

    (* initialize remaining season/oceans/crews *)
SeasonOceanShipSize[2] := SeasonOceanShipSize[1];
```

In the three-dimensional array, the crew sizes of all the ships for all seasons can be added together with a nested FOR loop.

```
sum := 0;
FOR i := 1 TO 2 BY 1 DO
  FOR j := 1 TO 4 BY 1 DO
    FOR k := 1 TO 5 BY 1 DO
      sum := sum + SeasonOceanShipSize[i,j,k];
    END;    (* FOR k *)
  END;    (* FOR j *)
END;    (* FOR i *)
```

To add together the crew sizes of all ships in the Indian Ocean for all seasons, you would write

```
sum := 0;
FOR i := 1 TO 2 BY 1 DO
  FOR k := 1 TO 5 BY 1 DO
    sum := sum + SeasonOceanShipSize[i,3,k];
  END;    (* FOR k *)
END;    (* FOR i *)
```

Finally, to add together the crew sizes of icebreakers for all oceans and seasons, you would write

```
sum := 0;
FOR i := 1 TO 2 BY 1 DO
  FOR j := 1 TO 4 BY 1 DO
    sum := sum + SeasonOceanShipSize[i,j,5];
  END;    (* FOR j *)
END;    (* FOR i *)
```

3.7 Summary/Problems

Arrays can model tabular information of virtually any form. Their role in programming is analogous to the role that tables and lists play in printed text—they are indispensable aids. Arrays allow large amounts of data to be conveniently accessed through one variable name. An entire array can be copied to another array with the *assignment operator* if the sizes, types, and index ranges of both arrays match. One exception to this rule is that strings can be assigned to longer CHAR arrays. In this case, null characters are appended to the character array to fill it out.

Because arrays are, by definition, collections of identical elements, processing them frequently requires repetition. Modula-2 handles repetition with a rich assortment of looping structures—in particular, REPEAT, WHILE, FOR, and LOOP. These instructions do overlap; what can be expressed in one can often be expressed in another. In general, FOR should be used in lieu of REPEAT or WHILE where appropriate, because it imparts clearer information to the human reader. Reserve LOOP for those special occasions calling for repetition without an exit condition or exit from the middle of a loop body.

Branching, or choosing between alternate paths of execution, is delegated to the IF and CASE statements. Because CASE is usually easier to understand than an equivalent IF, it is the preferred branching method.

Boolean expressions, the simplest consisting of two operands, such as a < b, provide the essential mechanisms for controlling branching and looping. Boolean variables have one of two values, TRUE or FALSE, and are ideal for expressing the dual conditions common in logic.

Problems

1. [L] What are the sizes in elements of arrays with the following dimension declarations:
    a. [1..5]
    b. [1..10]
    c. [−5..10]
    d. ARRAY[−5..5] OF
          ARRAY[−5..5]
    e. ARRAY[1..50] OF
          ARRAY[1..10] OF
          ARRAY[1..25]

2. [L] What is the value of the boolean expressions given in *a*, *b*, and *c* in the following?

   YoungAdmiral := TRUE;
   Mutiny := FALSE;

    a. (YoungAdmiral) AND Mutiny
    b. (NOT YoungAdmiral) OR Mutiny
    c. Mutiny AND (6 < 4)

3. [M] In which of the preceding is the value of the entire expression determined by the first operand alone?

4. [M] Write a program that converts Celsius temperatures to Fahrenheit and vice versa (Fahrenheit temperatures can be converted to Celsius using the equation F = 1.8C + 32). Specifically, request an integer value from the terminal keyboard and ask

   (C)Convert Celsius to Fahrenheit,
   (F)Convert Fahrenheit to Celsius,
   (Q)Quit?

   Continue accepting temperatures and converting them until the operator responds with a "Q." Echo the operator's replies and accept backspacing, upper and lower case, and reject invalid entries. Also maintain a counter of the number of conversions processed.

5. [M] Change the sample program Sortage to sort the crew ages in descending sequence (largest values first).

6. [S] In 1978, three scientists from the Massachusetts Institute of Technology published a report describing a public key encryption system using prime numbers. The system is called public because the encryption technique is not kept secret, as it is in most encryption methods, but can be revealed without compromising security. The system does require secrecy of the decryption procedure, which is a function of encryption.

   The success of this encoding algorithm lies in the difficulty of factoring large (100 digits or more) prime numbers. The algorithm is described in detail on page 120 of the February 1978 issue of *Communications of the Association for Computing Machinery*.

   Develop an algorithm for breaking this encryption scheme. If you're successful, contact the Central Intelligence Agency, National Security Agency, and the National Science Foundation, in that order.

4
Cargo
Organization

4. *Cargo Organization*

*A*s the cargo compartments of your program/ships become laden with data, you are faced with two problems: how to organize the cargo for efficient storage and how to streamline the increasingly complex logistical operations necessary to process such heavy loads. Modula-2 eases the way with the *type declaration* and *procedure* structures of the language. Both have been alluded to in previous chapters. You already know that several elementary types and procedures, especially those of the standard library module InOut, have had a role in most programs since the first launch.

Variables of a program resemble containers in a ship's hold; they store data just as containers store cargo. The different kinds of containers below deck confound the imagination. Jars, bottles, cans, cartons, and pouches of a plethora of sizes and shapes line the shelves and aisles. Engineers have designed these containers to meet the individual needs of the materials packaged. A dry, lightweight foodstuff like corn flakes carries well in a cardboard carton, but no one would think of putting five gallons of motor oil in a brown paper bag. A bag of oil would never survive the rigors of transoceanic travel, let alone a shot-put onto the shipping dock.

Modula-2 stocks a similar assortment of containers for every occasion. These containers are the variables that package the different kinds of data. The containers are specified by the *type* characteristic—such as INTEGER, CARDINAL, and REAL—that defines the size, shape, texture, and, ultimately, the use of a container/variable.

The number of container types has no limit because you can design your own containers as well as choose from a standard repertoire of off-the-shelf items. Selecting a container type is similar to deciding on a picture frame in a do-it-yourself frame shop. If you can't find the right frame in the stock selections for your *objet d'art*, then you can build your own in the back room.

Up to this point, the programs in this book have chugged along happily with the ready-made, factory-built types. Shortly, a visit to the back room, where types can be handcrafted to fit any size without wasted material, will be necessary.

The last sections of this chapter introduce procedures, the foot soldiers of Modula-2. Procedures afford you the opportunity to solve problems in piecemeal fashion—the strategy of divide and conquer. Virtually every significant program depends on procedures.

4.1 Why Types?

Few other languages mandate type declarations in the stringent fashion of Modula-2. Critics of Modula-2 (forgive their blasphemy) complain about the overhead required to keep checking that a variable remains within its type declaration. These skeptics embrace languages such as FORTRAN, COBOL, and assembly language, which could care less if you put castor oil in a container that used to have milk in it.

In the computer days of yore (translate 1950s), verifying the data integrity of a variable never crossed a language designer's mind. After all, there was barely room for a half-dozen variables in computer memory, let alone verification code. Programmers assumed responsibility for ensuring that variables were used in a compatible manner.

Today, and for at least the past decade, the argument of overhead no longer holds water. Computers with megabyte memories and giga-flop (one billion floating-point instructions per second) speeds are not dragged to their knees by checking variable types. Moreover, programmers need all the help they can get from a language when they are working with software

systems of tens or hundreds of thousands of statements. Type declarations give the compiler more information about the problem, and the compiler can use this information to check for errors and produce more efficient programs.

The critics of types fall mute in the face of failures of interplanetary space flights, train crashes, and false arrests that have actually been caused by programming bugs. Many of these failures could have been detected by a language, such as Modula-2, that requires explicit declaration of variable types and sizes.

LOST IN SPACE

Even the most trivial errors in using a language can sometimes lead to disastrous results. In a FORTRAN program controlling the United States' first mission to Venus, a programmer coded a DO statement in a form similar to the following:

DO 3 I = 1.3

The mistake he made was coding a period instead of a comma. [The FORTRAN statement DO 3 I = 1,3 is equivalent to the Modula-2 statement FOR I := 1 TO 3 BY 1.] However, the compiler treated this as an acceptable assignment statement because FORTRAN has no reserved keywords, blanks are ignored, and variables do not have to be explicitly declared. Although the statement is obviously an invalid DO statement, the compiler interpreted it as setting a new variable DO3I equal to 1.3. This "trivial" error resulted in the failiure of the mission. Of course, part of the responsibility for this billion-dollar error falls on the programmer and the test personnel, but is not the design of the FORTRAN language also partially to blame?

—Glenford J. Myers, *Software Reliability*, 1976.

4.2 TYPE *Declarations*

Ever since variables were introduced in chapter 2, the type has been declared in the VAR, or variable declaration, section of a module. For instance,

```
VAR
    NumFathoms,
    TotalInches : INTEGER;
```

declares variables NumFathoms and TotalInches as INTEGER.

An alternate way of indicating type is by declaring an *identifier* in the TYPE declaration section of a module and subsequently referring to that *identifier* or type name. The previous VAR declaration is equivalent to

```
TYPE
    scale = INTEGER;
VAR
    NumFathoms,
    TotalInches : scale;
```

In general, a declaration in the VAR section can be split into TYPE and VAR declarations. That is,

```
VAR
    SomeVar : SomeType;
```

is the same as

```
TYPE
    abc = SomeType;
VAR
    SomeVar : abc;
```

The primary advantage of a programmer-specified type name stems from the fact that the name can be referred to throughout the module to declare identical type variables. Later, if the scope of these variables must be changed, the modification can be accomplished by changing the one declaration of the type in the TYPE section.

For example, say four related variables are declared as CARDINAL in a different parts of a program:

```
VAR
    WaterTemp : CARDINAL;
    . . .
    CabinTemp : CARDINAL;
    . . .
    AirTemp : CARDINAL;
    . . .
    ShoreTemp : CARDINAL;
```

Later it is determined that these variables might assume negative values, so they must be changed to integers. Under the preceding scheme, each of the four declarations must be changed individually from CARDINAL to INTEGER.

If, on the other hand, a type declaration had been used, the types of all four variables could be modified with a single change in the type declaration. In other words, changing the variables in the statements

```
TYPE
    temp = CARDINAL;
VAR
    WaterTemp : temp;
    . . .
    CabinTemp : temp;
    . . .
    AirTemp : temp;
    . . .
    ShoreTemp : temp;
```

from CARDINAL to INTEGER requires only that the TYPE declaration temp = CARDINAL; be replaced with temp = INTEGER;. This technique is particularly beneficial when *subrange* types are involved, as will be demonstrated later in this chapter.

The types specified on the right side of a TYPE declaration need not be standard types. They can also be programmer-specified type names, such as

```
TYPE
    scale = INTEGER;
    depth = scale;
```

Progammer-specified type names on the right side of a TYPE declaration incur one restriction—they must have been previously declared. The statement sequence

```
TYPE
    depth  =  scale;
    scale  =  INTEGER;
```

violates this rule, because depth is declared as type scale, but scale wasn't yet declared.

Earlier, we stated that the type characteristic of a variable ensures that a variable is used only in operations and assignments that are compatible for that type. What constitutes type compatibility? The types of two variables are considered compatible if they are the same or if they are declared as equal. (The exception is that INTEGER and CARDINAL variables are assignment-compatible.) A variable is not boiled down to its fundamental type to determine compatibility. In the statements

```
TYPE
    HomePort   =  ARRAY [0..49] OF CHAR;
    SummerPort =  HomePort;
    WinterPort =  ARRAY [0..49] OF CHAR;
VAR
    SkiffDock : HomePort;
    BargeDock : WinterPort;
    DoryDock  : SummerPort;
```

variables SkiffDock and BargeDock are said to be incompatible, even though they are both arrays of 50 characters, because SkiffDock is of type HomePort and BargeDock is of type WinterPort. The assignment

```
    SkiffDock := BargeDock;
```

is *illegal.*

On the other hand, variables SkiffDock and DoryDock are compatible because the type SummerPort (of variable DoryDock) has been set equal to the type HomePort (of variable SkiffDock) in the TYPE declaration section. Thus, the assignment

```
    DoryDock := SkiffDock;
```

is legal.

Although SkiffDock and BargeDock are incompatible, their elements, which are of the type CHAR, are compatible, and the assignment

```
    BargeDock[i] := SkiffDock[j];
```

is legal.

To review, the TYPE declaration section is an optional part of a module, but it allows the programmer to name types. Named types often facilitate program maintenance.

4.3 Subranges

In previous examples, variables representing whole numbers could have theoretically ranged over the entire spectrum of integer or cardinal values, even though it was often clear in advance that the variable's actual value would extend over only a subrange of those values. For these cases, Modula-2 offers the type *subrange*, which allows you to define a type as a segment of a standard type.

For example, the statements

```
TYPE
    DayOfMonth = [1..31];          (* day of month *)
    FairbanksTemp = [-12..61];     (* Fairbanks, Alaska, average
                                      temperature range *)

    CapitalLetter = ["A".."Z"];    (* upper case letters *)
VAR
    dd : DayOfMonth;
    FairbanksWeather : FairbanksTemp;
    Initial : CapitalLetter;
```

declare three subranges. The first variable, dd, ranges from one to 31. During the program's execution, Modula-2 will confine dd to that range. If overflow (value greater than 31) or underflow (value less than one) occurs, the program is terminated with an appropriate error message.

The *base type* of a subrange determines the overall type. It may be declared either implicitly or explicitly. In implicit declarations, the base type corresponds to the values within brackets. For numeric subranges, a positive or 0 lower limit indicates type CARDINAL; a negative value indicates type INTEGER.

The base type of the subrange can be explicitly declared by prefixing an optional type identifier. Some examples of implicit and explicit declaration follow.

```
TYPE
    DayOfMonth  = [1..31];          (* implicit cardinal *)
    DayInMonth  = INTEGER[1..31];   (* explicit integer *)
    FairbanksTemp = [−12..61];      (* implicit integer *)
```

In DayOfMonth, the lower limit of the subrange is positive, so the base type is CARDINAL. DayInMonth, although having an identical subrange span, is of base type INTEGER because of the explicit declaration.

The type CapitalLetter (found in the example before this one) is a subrange of type CHAR. Its values range over the 26 upper-case letters of the alphabet, namely, "A," "B," "C," . . . "Z".

When subranges are used, two restrictions apply. First, subranges are not defined for REAL numbers. Second, subranges must not have gaps. The statements

```
TYPE
    JuneauTemp = [23.9..56.1];
    Vowels = ["A", "E", "I", "O", "U"];
```

are *illegal* for those reasons.

Operators that apply to variables of a particular type also apply to subranges of that type. Subranges may be mixed in expressions with subranges and other variables of the same base type without violating type-compatibility rules. Thus you could declare

```
TYPE
    LeftOver = [0..24];
    divamt = [1..25];
VAR
    extra : LeftOver;
    divisor : divamt;
    quantity : CARDINAL;
```

and then write the expression

```
extra := quantity MOD divisor;
```

To clarify the preceding points, the program AverageAge, introduced as Program 3–3 in chapter 3, has been modified to use subranges (see Program 4–1).

Program 4–1 AverageAge2

```
MODULE AverageAge2;        (* Calculate average age with type
                              declaration *)

FROM InOut IMPORT WriteLn,
                  WriteString,
                  ReadCard;
FROM RealInOut IMPORT WriteReal;

CONST
  CrewSize = 25;

TYPE
  CrewRange = [1..CrewSize];

VAR
  i : CrewRange;
  average : REAL;
  CrewAge : ARRAY CrewRange OF CARDINAL;

BEGIN
  WriteLn;
  WriteString("Enter crew ages: ");
  WriteLn;

  FOR i := 1 TO CrewSize BY 1 DO
    ReadCard(CrewAge[i]);                  (* get age from keyboard *)
    WriteLn;
  END;

  average := 0.0;
  FOR i := 1 TO CrewSize BY 1 DO      (* sum ages *)
    average := average + FLOAT(CrewAge[i]);
  END;

  average := average / FLOAT(CrewSize);    (* calculate average *)
  WriteLn;
  WriteString("Average age = ");
  WriteReal(average,10);
  WriteLn;

END AverageAge2.
```

The variable i of type CrewRange is a subrange, 1..CrewSize, of base type CARDINAL. Observe that the CrewRange subrange is also used to define the size of the array CrewAge. The statement

CrewAge : ARRAY CrewAge OF CARDINAL;

is equivalent to

CrewAge : ARRAY [1..25] OF CARDINAL;

If they have been designed with judicious use of types and constants, programs are much easier to modify and maintain. In the previous program, only the constant declaration

CrewSize = 25;

need be changed to modify the program for different crew sizes.

In general, the subrange type takes the form

subrange = [lowerbound..upperbound];

where the lower and upper bounds are constant expressions bounded by brackets and

lowerbound <= upperbound

Subranges need not be named but may be declared directly in the VAR section. The variable extra, for example, could be declared as

VAR
    extra : [0..24];

In most cases, however, it is preferable to declare the subrange type separately. Separate declaration allows the subrange name to be included in the compiler cross-reference and it also facilitates maintenance if more than one variable has the same subrange.

Subranges are the hallmarks of well-designed programs. In actual practice, few variables uncontrollably fluctuate over an entire base type, such as CARDINAL or INTEGER. Subranges provide more information to the human reader, resulting in programs that are easier to understand.

The compiler can also take advantage of range restrictions to detect erroneous assignments and produce more efficient programs.

4.4 Enumerations

Enumerations, like subranges, are a "roll-your-own" type. Enumeration types can be designed, invented, and created as necessary. As a programmer, you select the names that will be associated with these types; these names must be unique. Each name corresponds to an underlying cardinal value.

Some examples of enumeration types are

```
TYPE
    weekday = (Monday, Tuesday, Wednesday, Thursday, Friday);
    weekend = (Saturday, Sunday);
VAR
    workday,
    businessday : weekday;
    offday : weekend;
```

The variables workday and businessday can assume only one of five possible identifiers representing the days of the week. You could write an assignment as

```
workday := Wednesday;
```

Each value in an enumeration type corresponds to an underlying cardinal value starting at zero. These values can be accessed through the ORD standard function. For example,

```
ORD(Wednesday) = 2
ORD(Monday) = 0
ORD(Friday) = 4
```

Besides enumeration values, the ORD function also applies to enumeration variables. The statements

```
workday := Wednesday;
WriteCard(ORD(workday), 1);
```

display the cardinal value "2".

This example also illustrates a point of frequent confusion regarding enumeration input and output. It is not possible to directly display "Wednesday" for the variable workday. That is, a statement such as WriteString(workday), will cause the compiler to generate an error message because workday is *not* a string variable. The best you can do is display the enumeration's corresponding cardinal value with a statement such as WriteCard(ORD(workday), 1).

Three other standard functions in addition to ORD may be used with enumeration variables. Two of these have been employed with other types in earlier examples. If workday is set equal to Tuesday, then

```
INC(workday)            increment yields Wednesday
INC(workday,3)          increment by 3 yields Friday
DEC(workday)            decrement yields Monday
```

The other standard function, VAL, is the inverse of ORD. VAL(T,x) generates the value with ordinal number x of type T. For example,

```
workday :=  VAL(weekday,4);
```

assigns the value associated with the ordinal number 4 of type weekday, which in this case is Friday, to the variable workday.

The VAL function may also be used with types CHAR, INTEGER, and CARDINAL.

Among Modula-2's operators, only the assignment operator and relational operators apply to variables of type enumeration. An assignment takes the expected form

```
workday :=  businessday;
```

Relational expressions yield boolean values based on the defined enumeration order. Consequently, after the assignments

```
workday :=  Wednesday;
businessday :=  Friday;
```

the following expressions generate TRUE values.

```
workday < businessday
workday > Monday
```

Enumeration types can be incorporated into FOR loops as control variables. The sequence

```
FOR workday :=  Monday TO Friday BY 1 DO
   WriteCard(ORD(workday),2);
END;
```

would display 0, 1, 2, 3, 4.

The FOR statement above cannot be replaced by a WHILE statement. For example, the statements

```
workday := Monday;
WHILE workday <= Friday DO
    WriteCard(ORD(workday),2);
    workday := INC(workday);
END;
```

will fail when the expression INC(Friday) is evaluated because no successor to Friday was defined in the enumeration.

One enumeration type that has been used frequently in this book is the standard type BOOLEAN. Strictly speaking, this type is an enumeration with two values, namely,

```
BOOLEAN = (FALSE,TRUE);
```

and

```
ORD(FALSE) = 0
ORD(TRUE) = 1
```

To summarize, enumeration simply allows you to encode a sequence of cardinal values starting at 0 with more meaningful names. Using names rather than numbers often enhances readability. One implicit restriction regarding enumerations is that duplicate names are prohibited because they would lead to confusion. In other words, the type declarations

```
TYPE
    weekend = (Saturday,Sunday);
    holiday = (Friday,Saturday);
```

are *illegal* because the name Saturday appears in both.

4.5 Sets

SET types parallel the use of sets in mathematics. Sets are collections of related things or objects. A given object either is or is not a member of the set.

In Modula-2, sets define collections of values of a given *base type*. The base type *must be a subrange or enumeration*. For example, the statements

```
TYPE
    ZeroOne = [0..1];
    ingredients = (cocoa,coconut,sugar,butter,flour,eggs);
    BinaryNumbers = SET OF ZeroOne;
    confection = SET OF ingredients;
```

declare two sets: BinaryNumbers of base type ZeroOne is a CARDINAL subrange, and confection of base type ingredients is an enumeration.

The values of a set are its members enclosed by curly braces. The set members must be constant expressions. Variables are prohibited. For example, the possible values of the ZeroOne set are

```
{0}
{1}
{0,1}
{ }
```

Braces alone, as shown in this example, represent the empty set.

In general, if a base type has n distinct values, then its set type has 2 to the power of n values.

The sizes of sets are usually small, matching the word length of the computer used. On 16-bit systems, sets are typically restricted to 16 elements.

The operators associated with set variables are

+	set union
−	set difference
*	set intersection
/	symmetric set difference

Given the following variables (using the previously declared definition of type confection):

```
VAR
    topping,
    crust,
    filling,
    pie,
    fudge,
    cookie,
    sauce : confection;
```

the statements

```
topping   := confection{coconut,butter};
filling   := confection{cocoa,sugar,butter,flour,eggs};
crust     := confection{sugar,butter,flour};

pie       := topping + filling;
fudge     := filling − confection{butter};
cookie    := filling * crust;
sauce     := filling / crust;
```

yield

```
pie     = confection{coconut,butter,cocoa,sugar,flour,eggs};
fudge   = confection{cocoa,sugar,flour,eggs};
cookie  = confection{sugar,butter,flour};
sauce   = confection{cocoa,eggs};
```

The required prefix confection, before the set constants, explicitly matches the constants to a type identifier.

In the result of the set union operation, pie := topping + filling;, the common element is listed one time. That is, the ingredient butter appears in both topping and filling, but in the set union it is listed only once—you may not list the same element in a set more than once.

The symmetric set difference combines the unique values found in two sets. In other words, the set operation

a/b

is equivalent to

(a−b) + (b−a)

The assignment operator works as expected with sets. The statement

topping := confection{coconut,butter};

changes the variable topping to the set {coconut,butter}.

The relational operators that apply to sets are

=	equal
# or <>	not equal
<=	contained in (subset)
>=	contains (superset)
IN	membership of a single value

They yield a BOOLEAN value, TRUE or FALSE, depending on the outcome of the relation. For example, given the preceding operations involving the variables of type confection,

```
cookie = crust      produces TRUE
fudge # filling     produces TRUE
cookie <= filling   produces TRUE
fudge >= topping    produces FALSE
cocoa IN sauce      produces TRUE
```

Other examples are

```
{3} IN {1,2,3,4}        is TRUE
{2} IN {1,3}            is FALSE
{1} = {1,3}             is FALSE
{1,3} = {3,1}           is TRUE
{1,3} <= {1,2,3,4}      is TRUE
{1,3} <= {1,3}          is TRUE
{1,2,3,4} <= {1,3}      is FALSE
{ } <= {1,3}            is TRUE
```

Notice that the ordering of the elements within the set is irrelevant, that is, {1,3} = {3,1}. Also, the empty set is a subset of every set.

Modula-2 provides two standard procedures that deal exclusively with sets. INCL includes, or places, a single element into a set, and EXCL excludes, or removes, a single element from a set. Specifically,

```
INCL(s,i) is equivalent to s := s + {i};
EXCL(s,i) is equivalent to s := s - {i};
```

The element i may be any expression, constant or variable, matching the base type of set s.

For example, the statement

```
EXCL(filling,butter);
```

produces the same result as

```
filling := filling - confection{butter};
```

Within set, there is one predefined, standard type called BITSET. BITSET comprises the first w elements of the base type CARDINAL, where w is the word length of the computer being used. On 16-bit systems,

```
Numbers : BITSET;
```

is equivalent to

```
Numbers : SET OF [0..15];
```

Some legal values of this BITSET would be {∅}, {∅..1∅,13,14}, {7,8} and, as always, { }, or the empty set.

4.6 Procedures

Chapter 1 described a procedure as a collection of instructions that performs a particular action. Since that point in the book, procedures have been used extensively for terminal input and output, type conversions, and trigonometric operations. All of these procedures have been imported as canned routines from the module library.

Besides encapsulating commonly referenced routines, procedures serve as the building blocks of programs. Activities of complex programs can be assigned to different procedures. When the procedures have been completely written, they can be synergistically combined, as individual musical instruments blend to form a symphony.

Consider Program 4–2, which employs a procedure to perform exponentiation using the efficient square-and-halve algorithm. The program calculates x raised to the power y, where y is a cardinal value. Besides demonstrating simple procedures, this program illustrates the general outline of a MODULE:

```
MODULE heading
    constant declarations
    type declarations
    variable declarations
    procedure declarations
BEGIN
    module body
END
```

Although the syntax of a MODULE does not mandate this ordering, it is generally adhered to by convention. In any case, the declarations must always precede the module body.

Program 4–2 RaisePower

```modula2
MODULE RaisePower;        (* Raise x to the y power where y >= 0 *)
FROM InOut IMPORT WriteLn,
                  WriteString,
                  ReadCard;
FROM RealInOut IMPORT WriteReal,
                      ReadReal;

VAR
    z,                    (* accumulates result *)
    t,                    (* intermediate result *)
    x : REAL;             (* base from keyboard *)
    e,                    (* holds exponent *)
    y : CARDINAL;         (* exponent from keyboard *)

PROCEDURE Getxy;          (* get x & y from keyboard *)
  BEGIN
    WriteLn;
    WriteString("Enter x: ");
    ReadReal(x);
    WriteLn;
    WriteString("Enter y: ");
    ReadCard(y);
  END Getxy;

PROCEDURE Power;          (* raise x to y power *)
  BEGIN
    e := y;               (* initialize exponent *)
    t := x;               (* initialize intermediate result *)
    z := 1.0;             (* initialize result *)
    WHILE (e # 0) DO
      WHILE (NOT ODD(e)) DO
        t := t * t;
        e := e DIV 2;
      END;    (* WHILE NOT *)
      z := z * t;
      DEC(e);
    END;    (* WHILE e *)
  END Power;
```

```
PROCEDURE DisplayAnswer;
  BEGIN
    WriteLn;
    WriteString("x to y power = ");
    WriteReal(z,10);
    WriteLn;
  END DisplayAnswer;

BEGIN                          (* MODULE RaisePower *)
    WriteLn;
    WriteString("Calculating x to y power");
    Getxy;
    Power;
    DisplayAnswer;

END RaisePower.
```

When the program RaisePower is invoked (see Program 4–2), execution starts with the first statement in the *module body*; that statement is a call to the imported procedure WriteLn. *Calling* a procedure means executing the instructions contained in the procedure declaration.

The statements contained in the procedure Getxy are not executed until the third statement in the module body is executed. The first line of the procedure,

```
PROCEDURE Getxy;
```

is referred to as the *procedure heading*. The reserved word PROCEDURE declares the statements following it, up to END Getxy, as belonging to the procedure. The procedure name, Getxy, is a programmer-assigned *identifier*.

The *procedure body* starts with the BEGIN statement. Execution within the procedure body occurs sequentially, in the same manner as module bodies. After execution of the procedure, in this case after the ReadCard(y) statement, control returns to the statement following the procedure call.

The structure of procedures is virtually identical to that of modules. Constants, types, variables, and even other procedures can be defined within a procedure. Syntactically, procedures could pass for mirror images of modules, except that procedures begin with the reserved word PROCEDURE instead of MODULE.

The variables declared in a module are available to procedures within the module. These variables are aptly called global. Besides variables, global constants, types, and procedures can be used. The term *global identifiers* encompasses all of these.

Contrasting with global identifiers are *local identifiers*. Local identifiers are accessible only to the procedures in which they are defined. Procedures declared within a procedure also have access to local identifiers.

Local identifiers offer two distinct advantages over global identifiers:

1. They explicitly confine an identifier to its associated procedure, preventing unintentional access in other parts of the program.

2. They help minimize storage because local variables exist only while the procedure is active. The appropriate local variables are created when a procedure is invoked and disposed of when it is terminated.

In the program RaisePower, two of the variables—e and t—are used only in the procedure Power. Program 4–3 is a restructuring of the program RaisePower that shows how these variables can be declared local. In Program 4–3, variables e and t are visible only within the procedure Power. The visibility realm of an identifier is called its *scope*.

Program 4–3 RaisePower2

```
MODULE RaisePower2;        (* Raise x to y power (y >= 0) using local
                               variables *)

FROM InOut IMPORT WriteLn,
                  WriteString,
                  ReadCard;
FROM RealInOut IMPORT WriteReal,
                      ReadReal;

VAR
    z,                    (* accumulates result *)
    x : REAL;             (* base from keyboard *)
    y : CARDINAL;         (* exponent from keyboard *)

PROCEDURE Getxy;          (* get x & y from keyboard *)
    BEGIN
        WriteLn;
        WriteString("Enter x: ");
        ReadReal(x);
        WriteLn;
        WriteString("Enter y: ");
        ReadCard(y);
    END Getxy;
```

```
PROCEDURE Power;          (* raise x to y power *)
  VAR
    e : CARDINAL;         (* holds exponent *)
    t : REAL;             (* intermediate result *)
  BEGIN
    e := y;               (* initialize exponent *)
    t := x;               (* initialize intermediate result *)
    z := 1.Ø;             (* initialize result *)
    WHILE (e # Ø) DO
      WHILE (NOT ODD(e)) DO
        t := t * t;
        e := e DIV 2;
      END;      (* WHILE NOT *)
      z := z * t;
      DEC(e);
    END;        (* WHILE e *)
  END Power;

PROCEDURE DisplayAnswer;
  BEGIN
    WriteLn;
    WriteString("x to y power = ");
    WriteReal(z,1Ø);
    WriteLn;
  END DisplayAnswer;

BEGIN         (* MODULE RaisePower *)
  WriteLn;
  WriteString("Calculating x to y power");
  Getxy;
  Power;
  DisplayAnswer;

END RaisePower2.
```

Figure 4–1 helps illustrate procedure scopes; it shows procedure declarations and their corresponding scopes. The module or procedure(s) in which an identifier—type, constant, variable, or procedure—is visible depends on the module or procedure in which it was defined (see Table 4–1).

Given the scopes of these procedures, MODULE A may call PROCEDURES B and C. PROCEDURE B has access to PROCEDURE D, and PROCEDURE C has access to PROCEDURES E and F.

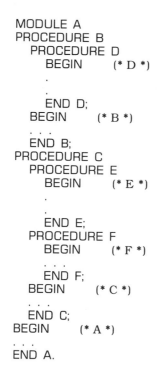

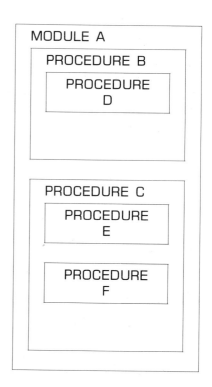

Figure 4–1

Table 4–1 The Module or Procedure(s) in Which an Identifier Is
Visible Depends on the Module or Procedure in Which It
Was Defined

Module or Procedure in Which Identifier Is Defined	Module or Procedure(s) in Which Identifier Is Visible
MODULE A	A, B, C, D, E, F
PROCEDURE B	B, D
PROCEDURE C	C, E, F
PROCEDURE D	D
PROCEDURE E	E
PROCEDURE F	F

Procedure calls on the same level are also possible. That is, PRO-CEDURES B and C may call each other. The same holds true for PROCEDURES E and F.

Because PROCEDURES D, E, and F are local, they cannot be called directly from the main module, MODULE A. MODULE A, however, can call PROCEDURE B, which may then call PROCEDURE D.

What happens when a global identifier has the same name as a local identifier? At first it may seem ambiguous, but Modula-2 tracks them as separate entities. Within the procedure, the local identifier takes precedence. Outside of the procedure, references to the identifer are made relative to that identifier's global definition.

Program 4–4 demonstrates what happens. In this case, the variable i is declared in both the main module and the procedure. This program displays

```
before procedure call, main i =      1
local i =     2
after procedure call, main i =      1
```

The rule of identifier precedence can be stated definitively as:

If an identifier *i* declared in a procedure *P* is redeclared in some inner procedure *Q* enclosed in *P*, then procedure *Q* and all procedures enclosed in *Q* are excluded from the scope of *i* declared in *P*. The definition of *i* within *Q* and its inner procedures reflects the redeclaration in *Q*.

Program 4–4 Main

```
MODULE Main;       (* Demonstrate use of duplicate identifiers *)

FROM InOut IMPORT WriteLn,
                  WriteString,
                  WriteInt;

VAR
   i : INTEGER;

PROCEDURE DisplayLocali;
   VAR
     i : INTEGER;
   BEGIN
     i := 2;          (* effects i only within this procedure *)
     WriteString("local i = ");
     WriteInt(i,5);
   END DisplayLocali;
```

```
BEGIN
  i := 1;

  WriteLn;
  WriteString("before procedure call, main i = ");
  WriteInt(i, 5);
  WriteLn;

  DisplayLocali;      (* call procedure *)

  WriteLn;
  WriteString("after procedure call, main i = ");
  WriteInt(i, 5);
  WriteLn;

END Main.
```

Procedure Parameters

So far, the procedures in this chapter differ from the standard procedures of module InOut in one primary respect. They are simple calls of the form

```
DisplayAnswer;
```

without *parameters*. Most of the procedures of InOut, and most procedures in general, include *parameter lists* in their calling statements. For example,

```
WriteInt(i, 5);
```

passes the parameters i and 5 to the procedure. They tell WriteInt what variable to display and what field width to use.

Perhaps the strongest asset of procedures is the ability to pass parameters. Through parameters, WriteInt has the flexibility to display integers in one, two, three, or more character fields. Essentially, parameters allow diversified activity from otherwise single-purpose groups of instructions.

Another revision of the program RaisePower—Program 4–5—illustrates the use of parameters in procedures. The three procedures of this program no longer refer to global variables. The interfacing between the procedures and the main module occurs solely through the procedure parameter lists.

The parameter lists in the procedure declarations are place holders for the actual variables supplied in the calling statement. In the procedure call

```
Getxy(x, y);
```

the variables x and y, called the *actual parameters*, are substituted for the *formal parameters*—base and exp—in the procedure heading. Subsequent accesses to base and exp in Getxy actually reference x and y. The formal parameters serve as symbols for the actual parameters that are passed to the procedure.

Program 4–5 RaisePower3

```
MODULE RaisePower3;      (* Raise x to y power ( y >= 0) using
                             procedure parameters *)

FROM InOut IMPORT WriteLn,
                  WriteString,
                  ReadCard;

FROM RealInOut IMPORT WriteReal,
                      ReadReal;

VAR
   z,                  (* receive result *)
   x : REAL;           (* base from keyboard *)
   y : CARDINAL;       (* exponent from keyboard *)

PROCEDURE Getxy(VAR base : REAL;   (* get x & y from keyboard *)
                VAR exp : CARDINAL);

   BEGIN
     WriteLn;
     WriteString("Enter x: ");
     ReadReal(base);
     WriteLn;
     WriteString("Enter y: ");
     ReadCard(exp);
   END Getxy;

PROCEDURE Power(t : REAL;              (* base *)
                e : CARDINAL;          (* exponent *)
                VAR xy : REAL);        (* result *)
   BEGIN
     xy := 1.0;                        (* initialize result *)
     WHILE (e # 0) DO
       WHILE (NOT ODD(e)) DO
         t := t * t;
         e := e DIV 2;
       END;     (* WHILE NOT *)
```

```
        xy := xy * t;
        DEC(e);
    END;      (* WHILE e *)
  END Power;

  PROCEDURE DisplayAnswer(xtoy : REAL);
    BEGIN
      WriteLn;
      WriteString("x to y power = ");
      WriteReal(xtoy,10);
      WriteLn;
    END DisplayAnswer;

  BEGIN      (* MODULE RaisePower *)
    WriteLn;
    WriteString("Calculating x to y power");
    Getxy(x,y);
    Power(x,y,z);
    DisplayAnswer(z);

  END RaisePower3.
```

Notice that the formal parameter's declaration in the procedure heading includes its type. This information enables the compiler to ensure that the variables passed match what the procedure expects. The calling parameters are matched to the procedure parameters sequentially (see Figure 4–2).

Having described the general characteristics of procedure parameters, let's dig into the particulars. Procedure parameters fall into two classes: *variable parameters* and *value parameters*.

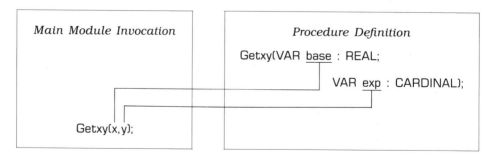

Figure 4–2

Variable Parameters

Conceptually, *variable parameters* are read/write parameters. They can be updated by the called procedure. The reserved word VAR preceding an identifier in the procedure heading indicates a variable parameter. Because changes made to variable parameters by the procedure also occur in the actual parameters of the calling module or procedure, variable parameters are often used to transmit results outside the procedure.

The procedure Getxy demonstrates the updating nature of variable parameters. The identifiers base and exp are synonyms for the actual parameters. Whatever happens to base and exp will also happen to x and y.

In general, the calling-statement parameters corresponding to variable parameters must be variables of the same type. Expressions and constants are not allowed. The statement

Power(2.0∗x,y,z);

is *illegal*, because the first parameter, which corresponds to a variable parameter in the procedure Power, is an expression.

The reserved word VAR in a procedure serves the dual purpose of indicating both variable parameters and variable declarations. Its meaning depends on the surrounding syntax, as shown here:

```
PROCEDURE SumUp(InArray : ARRAY[1..10] OF REAL;
                VAR Sum : REAL);      (* variable parameter *)
VAR
  i : CARDINAL;      (* variable declaration *)
```

Value Parameters

The second class of parameters, *value parameters*, conceptually resemble read-only parameters. The formal parameters of the procedure assume the values of the actual parameters of the calling statement. Regardless of what happens to the formal parameters within the procedure, the actual parameters remain unchanged.

Another way to picture value parameters is as copies. The actual parameters are copied to the formal parameters for use in the procedure.

In Program 4–5, procedure Power incorporates two value parameters. The lack of a VAR preface indicates value parameters, in this case t and e.

The procedure call

Power(x,y,z);

implicitly executes assignments for the value parameters:

```
t := x;
e := y;
```

Unlike variable parameters, value parameters may be variables, constants, or expressions. Furthermore, they need only be assignment-compatible with the procedure parameters. Thus, it is possible to write

```
Power(2.0*x, 15, z);
```

The Power procedure shows another attribute of parameters—that variable and value parameters may be mixed in a procedure heading. Other examples of parameter declarations are:

```
PROCEDURE ChkFuel(Distance,              (* value parm *)
    TankSize : CARDINAL;                 (* value parm *)
    WindSpeed : INTEGER);                (* value parm *)

PROCEDURE InitAll(VAR i : INTEGER;       (* variable parm *)
    VAR Abort : BOOLEAN;                 (* variable parm *)
    VAR BgnLet : CHAR;                   (* variable parm *)
    VAR Speed : REAL;                    (* variable parm *)
    VAR Name : ARRAY[1..8] OF CHAR);     (* variable parm *)

PROCEDURE ConDay(VAR JulDay : CARDINAL;      (* variable
                                                parm *)
    day : CARDINAL;                      (* value parm *)
    mm : ARRAY[1..9] OF CHAR);           (* value parm *)

PROCEDURE CalcAver(VAR average : REAL;   (* variable parm *)
    total : REAL;                        (* value parm *)
    VAR BadDiv : BOOLEAN);               (* variable parm *)
```

The exact order of declaration carries no significance, although it usually makes sense to group similar parameters together.

Overall, the decision to use variable or value parameters can be summarized by the following rule:

If the purpose of the procedure is to change the parameter, specify a VAR (variable) parameter in the procedure heading, otherwise, use a value parameter.

One exception to this rule may arise when large arrays are being passed to procedures. If a value parameter is used, a copy of the array is generated, consuming extra memory. Depending on the amount of memory available, it may be more prudent to use a variable parameter even though the procedure makes no changes to the array parameter.

Open Array Parameters

Another kind of parameter, which is actually a subset of variable and value parameters, is the *open array*. Open-array parameters are the same as regular array parameters except that the index range of the array is unspecified, or open. When this construct is used, arrays of any size may be passed to a procedure.

Take the problem of averaging the ages of a ship's crew. One way to express it in a procedure is

```
MODULE Average;
VAR
   CrewAge : ARRAY[1..25] OF CARDINAL;
   average : REAL;
. . .
PROCEDURE DoAverage (Ages : ARRAY [1..25] OF CARDINAL;
                          VAR CrewAverage : REAL);

   VAR
     i : CARDINAL;
   BEGIN
     CrewAverage := 0.0;
     FOR i := 1 TO 25 BY 1 DO
       INC(CrewAverage,FLOAT(Ages[i]));
     END;     (* FOR *)
     CrewAverage := CrewAverage / 25.0;
   END DoAverage;
. . .
BEGIN     (* MODULE Average *)
. . .
   DoAverage(CrewAge,average);
. . .
END AverageAge.
```

This formulation works, however, for only one size crew, namely, 25. To average a smaller or larger crew, another procedure would have to be written.

The open-array parameter instills a universal quality into procedures. With an open array, the procedure for averaging an array becomes

```
PROCEDURE DoAverage(Ages : ARRAY OF CARDINAL;
                        VAR CrewAverage : REAL);
   VAR
     i : CARDINAL;
```

```
BEGIN
  CrewAverage := 0.0;
  FOR i := 0 TO HIGH(Ages) BY 1 DO
    INC(CrewAverage,FLOAT(Ages[i]));
  END;     (* FOR *)
  CrewAverage := CrewAverage / 25.0;
END DoAverage;
```

This procedure works equally well for arrays of 10, 25, or 2500 elements. An analysis of the procedure will help reveal the distinguishing characteristics of open arrays.

First, observe the declaration of the Ages array in the procedure heading. It lacks an index range. The *absence of an index range* in a procedure heading array earmarks the parameter as an *open array*. The size of the array is implicitly passed to the procedure from the main module.

How does a procedure know the index range of an open array? Part of that question is easy—by definition, open arrays always start at element zero. For the upper index, the standard function HIGH is invoked. HIGH produces the upper bound of an array. The index range of an open array, say a, can be regarded as

[0..r]

where

r = HIGH(a);

If an array of the form

b : ARRAY [m..n] OF CHAR;

is passed to an open array, the index of the open array will be [0..(n—m)].

HIGH returns a cardinal value equal to the upper index of an array's first dimension. If the array is a null string or empty string, HIGH returns the value 0. That is,

HIGH(" ") = 0

HIGH may be used with regular arrays in addition to open arrays, but the result will not make sense if the upper bound is negative because HIGH produces a cardinal result. For example, with the array

c : ARRAY[−10..−5] OF CHAR;

HIGH(c) would generate an unpredictable value. As a rule, the standard function HIGH *should be applied only to open arrays or arrays whose upper index is non-negative.*

Referring again to the DoAverage procedure, the FOR statement demonstrates precisely how a procedure can access individual elements of an open array in a general manner. It starts with element 0, the first element of an open array (despite the array's original range declaration of [1..25] in the main module), and ends with HIGH(Ages), which in this case equals 24.

Regarding array operations, open arrays can be handled in the same manner as regular arrays, except that they cannot appear as units in assignment statements. Given the procedure heading

```
PROCEDURE ProcessAge(VAR Ages : ARRAY OF CARDINAL;
                     VAR NewAges : ARRAY OF CARDINAL);
```

the statement

```
Ages := NewAges;
```

is *illegal.*

Open arrays must be accessed element by element. They can, however, be passed as actual parameters to other procedures containing open array parameters. In other words,

```
PROCEDURE ProcessAge(Ages : ARRAY OF CARDINAL);
. . .
    PROCEDURE SortAge(InAges : ARRAY OF CARDINAL);
. . .
    END SortAge;
. . .
    SortAge(Ages);
. . .
END ProcessAge;
```

is perfectly legal.

Another restriction involves the number of dimensions in an open array. For all practical purposes, open arrays have one dimension and should serve as parameters only for other arrays with one dimension.

Open arrays expand the utility of procedures. They are indispensable to general-purpose math- and string-manipulation modules. For a prime example of this, look at the standard library module WriteString, which relies on an open array for input. Specifically, it is defined as

```
WriteString(s : ARRAY OF CHAR);
```

4.7 Function Procedures

Functions are a class of procedures that conveniently deliver results or computed values to expressions. Several of Modula-2's *standard functions* have already been used in this book. HIGH(a), for example, returns a cardinal value representing the upper bound of array a, and FLOAT(c) returns a real value representing the cardinal variable c.

Modula-2 permits you to supplement the standard repertoire with your own *function procedures*. Function procedures are declared in a manner similar to nonfunction, or *proper procedures*. Most of the procedures that have been referenced in the programs in this book—WriteLn and WriteString, for example—are proper procedures. The main differences between function and proper procedures are

1. Proper procedures return results through variable parameters or global variables. Functions directly return a result or computed value that may be used in an expression.

2. Functions are labeled by a type in the procedure heading that corresponds with the calling expression and returned result.

Program 4–6 shows the exact format of a function by implementing the exponentiation algorithm as a function procedure. Notice the similarities and differences between the declaration of the function procedure Power and the proper procedures cited in previous sections. First, a parameter list consisting of variables t and e, with their respective REAL and CARDINAL declarations follows the procedure name. This matches the format of the proper procedure declaration.

Program 4–6 RaisePower4

```
MODULE RaisePower4;        (* Raise x to y power (y >= 0) using
                              function procedure *)

FROM InOut IMPORT WriteLn,
                  WriteString,
                  ReadCard;
FROM RealInOut IMPORT WriteReal,
                      ReadReal;

VAR
    z,                      (* receives result *)
    x : REAL;               (* base from keyboard *)
    y : CARDINAL;           (* exponent from keyboard *)
```

```
PROCEDURE Getxy(VAR base : REAL;  (* get x & y from keyboard *)
                VAR exp : CARDINAL);
  BEGIN
    WriteLn;
    WriteString("Enter x: ");
    ReadReal(base);
    WriteLn;
    WriteString("Enter y: ");
    ReadCard(exp);
  END Getxy;

PROCEDURE Power(t : REAL;                   (* base *)
                e : CARDINAL) : REAL;       (* exponent *)
  VAR
    xy : REAL;                              (* holds result *)
  BEGIN
    xy := 1.0;                   (* initialize result *)
    WHILE (e # 0) DO
      WHILE (NOT ODD(e)) DO
        t := t * t;
        e := e DIV 2;
      END;     (* WHILE NOT *)
      xy := xy * t;
      DEC(e);
    END;     (* WHILE e *)
    RETURN xy;                   (* return result *)
  END Power;

PROCEDURE DisplayAnswer(xtoy : REAL);
  BEGIN
    WriteLn;
    WriteString("x to y power = ");
    WriteReal(xtoy,10);
    WriteLn;
  END DisplayAnswer;

BEGIN                             (* MODULE RaisePower *)
  WriteLn;
  WriteString("Calculating x to y power");
  Getxy(x,y);
  z := Power(x,y);
  DisplayAnswer(z);

END RaisePower4.
```

After the parameter list in the procedure heading, however, specifically after the closing parentheses, is another type declaration, in this case REAL. This type declaration refers to the result type of the function procedure. Appending a type name in this manner to a procedure declaration distinguishes the procedure as a function procedure as opposed to a proper procedure.

A local variable, xy, is defined for the result. This variable is explicitly returned as the value of the function by the last instruction in the function procedure, RETURN xy; .

RETURN serves two purposes: it assigns an expression to the function result and it terminates the function procedure, handing control back to the calling module or procedure. The type of the variable in the RETURN statement must match the type declared in the function procedure heading.

For example, the standard function FLOAT corresponds to an implicit declaration of the form

```
PROCEDURE FLOAT(c : CARDINAL) : REAL;
VAR
   r : REAL;
   . . .
   RETURN r;
END FLOAT;
```

Because functions return expressions, they can appear anywhere an expression is expected in a statement. Examples of legal use of functions follow:

```
solution := Power(9.34,5);
HairyOne := (sin(x) * Power(x,9)) / Power(x,3);
z := Power(FLOAT(c),y) + 26.2;
WriteReal(Power(3.14,y),10);
DisplayAnswer(Power(x,y));
```

The last example illustrates that the variable z, which is used to convey the result to the display routine in Program 4–6, can be eliminated.

A function procedure must be of an *unstructured* type. The unstructured types are INTEGER, CARDINAL, REAL, BOOLEAN, CHAR, subrange, and enumeration. Furthermore, subranges and enumerations must be named if they appear as function types. In other words, the declaration

```
PROCEDURE LeftOver(quantity : CARDINAL) : [0..5];
```

is *illegal*. It must be written as

```
TYPE
  residual = [0..5];
. . .
PROCEDURE LeftOver(quantity : CARDINAL) : residual;
```

Although only one value may be returned as the function expression, other values may be returned through variable parameters or global variables. For example,

```
PROCEDURE Mean(InNums : ARRAY OF REAL;
               VAR Total : REAL;
               VAR Size : CARDINAL;
               VAR NegNums : BOOLEAN) : REAL;
```

allows values to be returned through the variable parameters Total, Size, and NegNums, besides the function result. If a function incorporates variable parameters, though, it is usually better written as a proper procedure.

In the preceding examples, a single RETURN statement appeared last in the function. Although this location is appropriate, because RETURN does terminate the function, it is by no means a requirement. Moreover, in some cases an algorithm could be expressed better by locating the RETURN elsewhere or by using more than one RETURN.

RETURN can also be used to terminate a proper procedure at a point other than after the final statement. In these cases, RETURN frequently signals an abnormal termination. RETURN statements in proper procedures require no result expression. For example,

```
PROCEDURE ReadAndConvert(VAR Dec : CARDINAL;
                         VAR BadString : BOOLEAN);
. . .
  GetString(InData,Error);
  IF Error THEN
    BadString := TRUE;
    RETURN;
  END;    (* IF *)
  BadString := FALSE;
  ConvertString(InData,Dec);
END ReadAndConvert;
```

This procedure actually has two RETURNs: the RETURN in the IF statement and the implicit RETURN at the end of the procedure body.

The final point of syntax regarding functions involves the expression of an empty parameter list. Even if the function has no parameters, parentheses must be included with the declaration:

```
PROCEDURE Hour() : CARDINAL;
```

The calling statement follows the same convention. The presence of a parameter list distinguishes a function procedure call from a variable reference. For example,

```
hh := Hour();     (* call a function procedure named Hour *)
hh := Hour;       (* reference a variable named Hour *)
```

The use of parentheses in parameterless functions differs from non-function procedures. The standard procedure for displaying a line feed/carriage return, which has no parameters, is written without parentheses as

```
WriteLn;
```

4.8 Summary/Problems

Types are the taxonomy of Modula-2. They determine the genera and species of variables. Animals and variables share two qualities: they do not switch species during a lifetime, and they generally interact only with members of the same species.

The types introduced in this chapter strengthen Modula-2's data-handling capabilities. Subranges offer the advantages of:

1. Self-documentation—they help convey the purpose of a variable.

2. Efficiency—the compiler can deal with restricted ranges more economically.

3. Protection—they prevent variables from assuming incorrect values because of unforeseen circumstances.

Enumerations enhance readability by assigning identifiers to cardinal values.

Sets are useful for describing collections of objects.

Typical uses for the different types are shown in Table 4–2.

Table 4–2 Typical Uses for the Different Types

Type	Typical Use
CARDINAL	Counters and indexes with positive only values
INTEGER	Counters and indexes with both positive and negative values
REAL	Numbers with fractional parts and very large or very small numbers
BOOLEAN	Answers to true or false and yes or no questions
CHAR	Text to be displayed or printed
Subrange	Numbers or characters that fall within a specific range, such as 0 to 9 or A to Z
Enumeration	Small lists, such as the days in a week, months in the year, or colors in the rainbow
ARRAY	Tables of numbers or strings of characters
SET	Collections of similar objects, such as ingredients in a recipe

The balance of the chapter explained procedures and function procedures. Most programming applications, like recipes, consist of a series of steps. Procedures neatly enclose the individual steps.

Communication between modules and procedures occurs at three levels. First, data may be passed at a global level. *Global variables* are accessible to all parts of a module.

Second, *value parameters* communicate in one direction. Essentially, value parameters cause copies of variables to be sent to a procedure. Mod-

ifications made to the value parameter by the called procedure do not affect the associated variable in the calling module or procedure.

Third, *variable parameters* correspond with data items that *vary*. These parameters are commonly used to convey the results of a procedure calculation or process.

Function procedures differ from *proper procedures* in that a result is returned as an expression. A function's type limits its use to expressions of a compatible type.

ODE TO A TYPE

There can be hype
About all these types.
It might seem trite
To declare every byte,
But in other light,
They make your code tight.
So rather than fight,
Give thanks for the types.

—E. J.

Problems

1. [L] What is the base type of the following subranges?

```
ArcticTemp = [−50..75];
MenuSelection = [1..10];
HexDigits = ["A".."F"];
```

2. [L] Given the enumerations

   TYPE
      color = (red,white,blue);
      suits = (clubs,diamonds,spades,hearts);
      processor = (z80,i8086,m68000,n16000,nec7500);

   what do the following expressions yield?

   VAL(suits,3)
   ORD(white) = ORD(i8086)   (* true or false? *)
   ORD(red)

3. [M] The procedure Power in Program 4–6 raises a real value to a positive integer power. Modify the procedure to accept any integer value, positive or negative, as the power. It may help to remember that

   $$x^{-n} = 1.0/x^n$$

4. [M] In the Power procedure, the solution will be undefined if x and y are both 0. Add logic to the procedure to test x and y to find out if either one is 0; then return a BOOLEAN variable parameter, CanDo. Set CanDo to TRUE if the power can be evaluated. Otherwise, set it to FALSE.

5. [D] From doing problems 3 and 4, you now have a fairly generalized exponentiation procedure. It lacks only a solution for the situation in which the power is nonintegral, that is, the power contains a fraction. For this case, the formula

   $$x^y = \exp(\ln(x) * y);$$

   where exp and ln are standard procedures from module MathLib0, is recognized as the one of the most efficient calculations of x^y. The only restriction is that x must be positive or the result will be an imaginary number.

   Add this formula to the Power procedure and rely on it for the specific case just described. When x is negative, set CanDo to FALSE and exit from the procedure.

5.
High
SeaS
Cruising

5. High-Seas Cruising

$\mathcal{M}$ost of the Modula-2's elementary concepts have now been discussed. The more specialized tools of the language lay ahead; they will enable the range of sea-going journeys to be expanded.

The topics to be discussed in this chapter include recursion (the capability of a procedure to activate itself); more sophisticated forms of I/O (input and output); the standard type RECORD and its subform, RECORD variant; and POINTER and PROCEDURE types.

5.1 Recursion: See Recursion

The section on procedures in chapter 4 explained that a procedure may call other procedures that are declared at the same level. But can procedures call themselves? Indeed they may. The self-activation of a procedure is termed *recursion*.

Recursive procedures resemble recursive definitions. Take the word *descendant*, for example:

A descendant of a person is a son or daughter of the person, or a descendant of the son or daughter.

Although the word *descendant* recurs in the definition, the end result is more concise than

A descendant of a person is a son or daughter of the person, or a grandson or granddaughter of the person, or a great-grandson or great-granddaughter of the person, etc.

Similarly, some programming applications best fit a recursive scheme. The classic examples are polynomial mathematical expressions in which the solutions are determined by application of formulas to preceding terms.

Recursive procedures in Modula-2 require no special declaration format or syntax. They are defined just as normal procedures are. Whether a procedure calls itself or not makes no difference to Modula-2.

As an example, consider the problem of adding the n elements of an integer array. Using recursion, the sum could be calculated as the last element added to the sum of the first $n - 1$ elements. The recursive function procedure Sum expresses the formula:

```
PROCEDURE Sum(a : ARRAY OF INTEGER;
                  n : CARDINAL) : INTEGER;
BEGIN
  IF (n = 1) THEN
    RETURN a[Ø];
  ELSE
    RETURN (a[n-1] + Sum(a,n-1));
  END;      (* IF *)
END Sum;
```

If a were a four-element array with the values 7, 1, 9, and 5, the procedure call Sum(a,4) would generate four procedure calls. Execution of the procedure would occur as shown in Table 5–1.

Theoretically, any recursive procedure can be expressed as an iterative or repetitive scheme. Sum, for example, simply becomes

```
Total := Ø;
FOR i := Ø TO n-1 BY 1 DO
  Total := Total + a[i];
END;
RETURN Total;
```

In the case of adding an array, iteration solves the problem more elegantly. Iteration also offers the advantage of less overhead than procedure calls.

Understanding recursion constitutes only part of the task of implementing recursive procedures. The other part lies in knowing when to

Table 5-1 Execution Flow of Recursive Procedure Sum(a,4)

Depth of Recursive Call	Value of Sum
1	Sum(a,4)
2	5 + Sum(a,3)
3	5 + (9 + Sum(a,2))
4	5 + (9 + (1 + Sum(a,1)))
4	5 + (9 + (1 + 7))
3	5 + (9 + 8)
2	5 + 17
1	22

choose recursion over iteration. In general, recursive techniques are employed only if they condense and clarify an algorithm better than an equivalent iterative expression.

The final note regarding recursion involves protocol. Procedures may call themselves through other procedures. That is, procedure A calls procedure B, which then calls procedure A. This chain of calls is perfectly legal, provided, of course, that the procedures fall within the prerequisite scopes.

5.2 Sequential File Access

How well a language handles external data files can determine success or failure on the high seas of computing. For starters, Modula-2 provides sequential file access in a standard library module. Sequential access is straightforward. It uses the same procedures employed for terminal screen and keyboard access.

File Creation

Program 5-1, FileMake, demonstrates creation of a file with 100 entries. The entries are written in the format

characters 1–8	crew member number (cardinal value)
characters 9–34	crew member job description
	(initially filled with characters A–Z)

Program 5–1 FileMake

```
MODULE FileMake;      (* Sequential file creation *)

FROM InOut IMPORT EOL,        (* end of line *)
                  Done,        (* status of operation
                                  TRUE => success
                                  FALSE => failure *)
                  OpenOutput,  (* accept file name from terminal
                                  & open it for output *)
                  CloseOutput, (* close output file *)
                  Write,       (* write character *)
                  WriteCard,   (* write cardinal value *)
                  WriteLn,     (* write cr/line feed *)
                  WriteString; (* write string *)
CONST
  JobDes = "ABCDEFGHIJKLMNOPQRSTUVWXYZ";
VAR
  CrewNum : [1..100];
```

```
BEGIN
   WriteString("Enter output file name: ");

   REPEAT
      OpenOutput(" ");       (* supply no default extension *)
   UNTIL Done;

   FOR CrewNum := 1 TO 100 BY 1 DO
      WriteCard(CrewNum,8);
      WriteString( JobDes);
      Write(EOL);
   END;

   CloseOutput;
   WriteString("File creation complete");
   WriteLn;

END FileMake.
```

On the surface, this program looks like a program designed to access the terminal screen. Without execution of the procedure OpenOutput, the program *would* access the terminal screen.

An examination of FileMake will help explain this type of file manipulation.

As was discussed earlier, module InOut can be called upon for terminal access; here, however, it is being employed to process a file. How does Modula-2 determine if execution of a WriteString procedure, for instance, is meant for the terminal screen or for a file?

The procedures within InOut assume that output will go to the terminal screen unless the procedure OpenOutput is executed. OpenOutput requests a file name from the terminal keyboard and opens that file for output. Subsequent output through InOut is directed to the file instead of to the terminal screen. The redirection remains in effect until the CloseOutput procedure is executed, at which time output is returned to the terminal screen.

In the program FileMake, what actually appears on the terminal screen from the time the program starts until it finishes is

Enter output file name: out>
File creation complete

The message, "Enter output file name: " is generated by the first WriteString statement in the program. The OpenOutput procedure call, which follows two statements later, displays the prompt "out>" and requests a file name.

The general form of OpenOutput is

OpenOutput(defext : ARRAY OF CHAR);

The variable defext represents a character array that supplies a default file extension if none is entered by the terminal operator. The default extension is appended to the file name only if the file name ends with a period.

For example, if

OpenOutput("TXT");

were executed and the operator entered "TEST.", then OpenOutput would automatically append the extension, creating the file TEST.TXT. On the other hand, if the operator entered "TEST.SRC", then the default extension would be ignored.

Program 5–1 specified a null string with the statement

OpenOutput(" ");

This means that file names entered as "TEST." are created with that name only and no extension.

A REPEAT loop surrounds the OpenOutput call in case the operator enters an invalid file name. Exit from the loop depends on a successful file opening. The boolean variable Done, imported from InOut, indicates the status of the operation. If the file was successfully opened, it is set TRUE.

When OpenOutput obtains a valid name, the file is created in the disk directory. If the file already exists, it will be overwritten. The program then writes 100 34-character entries to the file. EOL, imported from InOut, indicates the end of each entry. Identifiers EOL and Done demonstrate that constants and variables, as well as procedures, can be imported from outside modules.

File Copying

Program 5–2 demonstrates the use of file input and output with module InOut. It copies the entire contents of one file to another file. The bulk of FileCopy resembles FileMake. The procedures OpenInput and OpenOutput prompt the operator for input and output files.

After the files are opened, the program reads the input file one character at a time and writes the character to the output file. Following each read, the file-status switch, Done, is tested. Done is set FALSE by InOut if the end of the input file is reached upon executing a Read procedure. At the completion of the program, the number of lines copied is displayed on the terminal screen.

Module InOut sequentially processes one input and/or one output file in a simple, straightforward manner. For multifile processing, extensive error checking, and random access, the module FileSystem, which is described later in this chapter, must be used.

Program 5–2 FileCopy

```
MODULE FileCopy;      (* File copy *)

FROM InOut IMPORT EOL,            (* end of line *)
                  Done,           (* status of operation
                                     TRUE => success
                                     FALSE => failure *)
                  OpenInput,      (* accept file name from terminal
                                     & open it for input *)
                  OpenOutput,     (* accept file name from terminal
                                     & open it for output *)
                  CloseInput,     (* close input file *)
                  CloseOutput,    (* close output file *)
                  Read,           (* read character *)
                  Write,          (* write character *)
                  WriteCard,      (* write cardinal value *)
                  WriteString;    (* write string *)

VAR
   LinesCopied : CARDINAL;  (* counts lines copied *)
   ch : CHAR;               (* character read/written *)

BEGIN
   WriteString("Enter input and output file names: ");
   REPEAT                        (* get input file *)
      OpenInput(".IN");          (* supply default extension *)
   UNTIL Done;

   REPEAT                        (* get output file *)
      OpenOutput(".OUT");        (* supply default extension *)
   UNTIL Done;

   LinesCopied := Ø;             (* initialize lines copied counter *)

   LOOP
      Read(ch);                  (* read character from in file *)
```

```
        IF (NOT Done) THEN        (* read operation successful? *)
            EXIT;                 (* no—must be end of file, quit *)
        END;     (* IF *)
        Write(ch);                (* yes—write char to out file *)
        IF (ch = EOL) THEN        (* character = end of line? *)
            INC(LinesCopied);     (* yes—increment lines copied *)
        END;     (* IF *)
    END;      (* LOOP *)          (* perform next read *)

    CloseOutput;
    CloseInput;
    WriteString("File copy complete ");
    WriteCard(LinesCopied,5);
    WriteString(" lines copied");

END FileCopy.
```

5.3 *Type* RECORD

In many programming environments, the term *record* refers to a logical entity in a file, especially a disk file. In Modula-2, the type RECORD may encompass file entities, but it actually defines a much broader data structure.

The type RECORD resembles ARRAY; both are structured types with several components. The types differ, however, in how these components are accessed and constructed. Whereas array components are accessed by subscripts and must be of the same type, record components are accessed by name and may be composed of disparate types.

For example, a data structure describing a sailboat could be declared as

```
TYPE
    sailboat =
      RECORD
        masts : [1..5];
        yearsold : CARDINAL;
        catamaran : BOOLEAN;
        skippername : ARRAY[0..24] OF CHAR;
      END;
```

This declaration defines a RECORD type, sailboat, consisting of four components. The reserved words RECORD and END enclose the body of the record. The record components are formatted in a manner similar to variable declarations.

Variables of type sailboat are declared in the usual way, namely,

```
VAR
    schooner,
    frigate : sailboat;
```

Individual components of record variables are accessed through *record selectors* comprised of the variable name followed by the record field name. For example,

```
schooner.skippername := "John Paul Jones";
IF (frigate.masts = 4) THEN
    . . .
```

Record types, like arrays, can be composed of other structured types, as just illustrated. To access the eighth element of the array skippername in the record schooner, the statement

```
schooner.skippername[7] := "u";
```

can be written.

Conversely, arrays may be comprised of record types:

```
VAR
    fleet : ARRAY[1..100] OF sailboat;
```

declares 100 elements of type sailboat, and

```
fleet[38].skippername[7] := "u";
```

assigns the character *u* to the eighth position of skippername in the 38th element of fleet.

Like arrays, entire records can be manipulated as units, as long as the base types of their components agree. For example,

```
schooner := frigate;
```

is equivalent to

```
schooner.masts        := frigate.masts;
schooner.yearsold     := frigate.yearsold;
schooner.catamaran    := frigate.catamaran;
schooner.skippername  := frigate.skippername;
```

The assignment operator is the only operator that may be used on records as units. Statements using relational operators of the form

```
IF (schooner = frigate) THEN
```

are *illegal*.

Another attribute records share with arrays is nesting, as the statements that follow illustrate:

```
TYPE
  date =
    RECORD
      mm : [1..12];      (* month *)
      dd : [1..31];      (* day *)
      yy : [0..99];      (* year *)
    END;
  trawler =
    RECORD
      tons : CARDINAL;
      launchdate : date;
      diesel : BOOLEAN;
      skippername : RECORD
                      fname : ARRAY[0..11] OF CHAR;
                      minit : CHAR;
                      lname : ARRAY[0..11] OF CHAR;
                    END;
    END;
VAR
  shrimpboat : trawler;
```

To access individual components of the record shrimpboat, we extend the *record selector*. For example,

```
shrimpboat.launchdate.mm := 9;
shrimpboat.skippername.minit := "P";
```

The hierarchical structure of this record is shown in Figure 5–1.

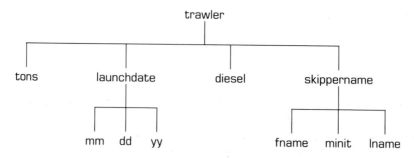

Figure 5–1 The Hierarchical Structure of the Record shrimpboat

Assuming that the type trawler is declared in the same program as type sailboat, this example also demonstrates that identical field names may be used in different records. Because the record selector ties the field name to a variable, the field skippername corresponds to a subrecord in variables of type trawler, but in variables of type sailboat it corresponds to a 25-character array. Naturally, identical field names within the same record would lead to ambiguity and are thus prohibited.

WITH

Prefixing the names of record variables to fields can sometimes lead to wordy programs. Modula-2 provides a way to reduce this wordiness through the WITH statement. WITH is to records what the FOR statement is to arrays. In particular,

```
WITH schooner DO
    masts := 3;
    yearsold := 15;
    catamaran := FALSE;
    skippername := "Black Beard";
END;
```

is equivalent to

```
    schooner.masts := 3;
    schooner.yearsold := 15;
    schooner.catamaran := FALSE;
    schooner.skippername := "Black Beard";
```

Like FOR statements, WITH statements may be nested:

```
WITH shrimpboat DO
    WITH launchdate DO
        mm := 9;
        dd := 14;
        yy := 51;
    END;    (* WITH launchdate *)
END;    (* WITH shrimpboat *)
```

Each WITH accepts one variable reference. Statements of the form

```
WITH shrimpboat, launchdate DO
    . . .
```

are *illegal*.

Another restriction involves the statements bounded by the WITH: these statements must not change with WITH variable. Improved efficiency results from this rule, because the compiler need only evaluate the WITH variable once. The following statements show a violation of this restriction:

```
WITH schooner DO
    masts := 3;
    schooner := frigate;    (* this assignment changes the WITH
                                variable *)
END;
```

At best, the result is obscure. At other times, it may be unpredictable. Consequently, WITH statement sequences that change the WITH variable should be avoided.

5.4 RECORD *Variants*

One of the main differences between records and arrays stems from the constitution of individual elements. Elements in arrays must all be of one type. Record elements, on the other hand, may be comprised of nonuniform types.

The gulf separating these two structured data types grows even wider when RECORD variants come into play. This breed of RECORD adds a new dimension to data structures. Not only can elements within the RECORD include diverse types, but they can dynamically assume different size and shape variables based on the data in the RECORD.

Simple Example of a Variant

Suppose you want to store data on the engine displacement of a ship. On small craft, the displacement is expressed in cubic centimeters (cc) as an integral number, for example, 1800 cc. On large ships, the displacement is expressed in liters with a fractional part, for example, 3.6 liters.

One option for storing this data would be a single record with each item. That is,

```
TYPE
   engine =
     RECORD
        SmallCraft : BOOLEAN;        (* TRUE implies small craft,
                                        FALSE implies large ship *)

        SizeCC : CARDINAL;
        SizeLiter : REAL;
     END;
```

This record solves the problem of covering the incongruous possibilities, but it stores an extra field. If the ship is small, the field SizeLiter will not be used. Similarly, field SizeCC will not be used for large ships. In hundreds or thousands of records, the extra fields add up to a significant amount of wasted space.

Fortunately, we can tailor record types to these nonuniform situations with RECORD variants. The following example shows how RECORD variants streamline the declaration of type engine.

```
TYPE
   engine =
     RECORD
        CASE Smallcraft : BOOLEAN OF
          TRUE : SizeCC : CARDINAL; |
          FALSE : SizeLiter : REAL;
        END;      (* CASE *)
     END;     (* RECORD *)
```

This record consists of two parts: a *fixed* part and a *variant* part. The fixed part is comprised of the field SmallCraft, which indicates whether or not a ship is small. This boolean field will appear in all records of type engine, for both small craft and large ships.

The value of the *tag field* determines the format of the remaining part of the record, or variant part. The tag field (variable SmallCraft, in this case) is designated by the CASE clause. Until the tag field has been assigned—that is, until the tag field assumes a value during execution of the program—the variant part is considered to be undefined.

For example, given the declaration and assignment

```
VAR
   motor : engine;
   . . .
   motor.SmallCraft := TRUE;
```

the statement

```
IF (motor.SizeCC = 1800) THEN
   . . .
```

could be written.

Alternatively, given the assignment

```
motor.SmallCraft := FALSE;
```

the following expression could be written:

```
IF (motor.SizeLiter > 3.6) THEN
   . . .
```

The value of the tag field, SmallCraft, effectively controls the format of the remaining part of the record. If SmallCraft is TRUE, the variant part consists of a CARDINAL field, SizeCC. If SmallCraft is FALSE, the variant part consists of REAL field SizeLiter. The variant possibilities are mutually exclusive. In a given record, one or the other will apply, but not both.

The CASE part of a record variant closely parallels the CASE instruction for choosing alternate actions. Hence, the processing of a record variant often fits best in a CASE statement. For example, if the following array of records is declared:

```
FleetMotors : ARRAY[1..100] OF engine;
```

the succeeding program segment would process the variant information:

```
FOR i := 1 TO 100 BY 1 DO
   WITH FleetMotor[i] DO
      WriteLn;
      CASE Smallcraft OF
         TRUE : WriteString("CC Size = ");
                WriteCard(SizeCC,8); |
         FALSE : WriteString("Liter Size = ");
                 WriteReal(SizeLiter,8);
      END;      (* CASE *)
   END;      (* WITH *)
END;      (* FOR *)
```

Complex Example of a Variant

A more complicated and perhaps more realistic example of record variants could be written regarding the storage of data on three types of ships: sailboats, trawlers, and tugboats. Boilerplate information for each ship—plus three, four, or five other items, depending on the kind of ship—is available. The boilerplate information is

tons

name

age (years old)

ship kind

Additionally, the ship data includes a commission date whose format varies according to the ship's age:

0–10 years	*11–30 years*	*> 30 years*
mm/dd/yy	mm/yy	yy

Other items, according to the class of ship, are

sailboat	*trawler*	*tugboat*
number of masts	diesel (true or false)	engine size
catamaran (true or false)	hold size	length
manufacturer		width
		harbor

The following example shows how RECORD variants encapsulate this data:

```
TYPE
shipkind = (sailboat,trawler,tugboat);
shipinfo =
  RECORD
    tons : CARDINAL;
    name : ARRAY[1..20] OF CHAR;
    CASE yearsold : CARDINAL OF
      0..10 : mm : [1..12];
              dd : [1..31];
              yy : [0..99]; |
      11..30 : mm : [1..12];
               yy : [0..99];
        ELSE : yy : [0..99];
    END;    (* CASE yearsold *)
```

```
CASE whatship : shipkind OF
  sailboat : masts : [1..5];
             catamaran : BOOLEAN;
             manufacturer : ARRAY[1..15] OF CHAR; |
  trawler : diesel : BOOLEAN;
            holdsize : CARDINAL; |
  tugboat : enginesize : CARDINAL;
            length,
            width : REAL;
            harbor : ARRAY[1..15] OF CHAR;
  END;      (* CASE whatship *)
END;      (* RECORD *)
```

The fixed part consists of the fields tons, name, yearsold, and whatship. Fields yearsold and whatship control the format of the two variant parts. The values later assigned to yearsold and whatship determine the structure of these variant parts of the record.

If the yearsold field of a shipinfo type variable contains the value 9, the commission date will consist of the fields mm, dd, and yy; if it contains the value 11, the date will consist of the fields mm and yy; if it contains the value 31, the date will consist only of the field yy.

If this array of records is declared:

```
fleet : ARRAY[1..50] OF shipinfo;
```

the following program segment would process the fixed part of field name and part of the variant information covered by whatship:

```
FOR i := 1 TO 50 BY 1 DO
  WITH fleet[i] DO
    WriteLn;
    WriteString("ship name = ");
    WriteString(name);
    CASE whatship OF
      sailboat : WriteString("--sailboat--");
                 WriteString("masts = ");
                 WriteCard(masts, 1); |
      trawler : WriteString("--trawler--");
                WriteString("hold size = ");
                WriteCard(holdsize, 3); |
      tugboat : WriteString("--tugboat--");
                WriteString("engine size = ");
                WriteCard(enginesize, 5);
```

```
    END;      (* CASE *)
  END;      (* WITH *)
END;      (* FOR *)
```

To summarize, three rules govern the use of record variants:

1. A record can have several variant parts. Each part terminates with an END statement.

2. The tag field must be declared as type INTEGER, CARDINAL, BOOLEAN, CHAR, subrange, or enumeration. Subranges and enumerations must be named and defined previously—they cannot be declared directly. Thus, the statement

```
TYPE
  month = [1..12];
  birthday =
    RECORD
      CASE mm : month OF
```
. . .

is legal, but

```
TYPE
  birthday =
    RECORD
      CASE mm : [1..12] OF
```
. . .

is *illegal*.

3. Since record variants are a category of RECORD, they can be nested like RECORD types.

5.5 *Random File Access*

Module InOut furnishes procedures for sequential file processing, but it has no provisions for random access, multifile processing, or extensive error checking. To address those applications, it is necessary to resort to the sophisticated mechanisms found in the library module FileSystem.

Strictly speaking, a Modula-2 complier need not support FileSystem because it is not part of the language definition. Most systems include it, however, because it was implemented in the original Modula-2 compiler on the Lilith computer and it provides the only vehicle for random file access.

Random file access allows the entries of a file to be read or written in arbitrary order. In other words, to read the 32nd entry in a file, it is possible to simply move to it and perform a read operation. Sequential access, on the other hand, requires that the 31 preceding entries be read first.

The difference between random and sequential access resembles the difference between stereo albums and cassette tapes. To play a particular musical recording on an album, the turntable needle need only be positioned to the desired track. To play the recording on tape, it is necessary to *sequentially* move the tape past preceding recordings.

Program 5–3 is an example of random file access using FileSystem. The program updates a crew member's job description in two redundant files that match the format created in the sequential-processing program of section 5.2.

Program 5–3 FileUpdt

```
MODULE FileUpdt;      (* Update two files using random access *)

(* terminal input/output *)
FROM InOut IMPORT ReadCard,        (* read cardinal value *)
                  ReadString,      (* read string *)
                  WriteLn,         (* write cr/line feed *)
                  WriteString;     (* write string *)

(* file input & output tools *)
FROM FileSystem IMPORT File,       (* file definition *)
                  Response,        (* includes 'done' *)
                  Lookup,          (* look up file on disk *)
                  SetModify,       (* set modify mode *)
                  SetPos,          (* set position *)
                  Close,           (* close *)
                  ReadChar,        (* read character *)
                  WriteChar;       (* write characer *)
```

```
CONST
  LenCrData = 36;        (* length of data per crew member in file,
                             includes carriage return/line feed *)
  LenCrNum = 8;          (* length of crew mem number in file *)
VAR
  FL1,
  FL2 : File;                        (* contains file definition &
                                        status info *)
  CrewNum : [1..100];                (* crew mem. number *)
  JobDes : ARRAY[0..25] OF CHAR;     (* job description *)

(* Initialize file *)
PROCEDURE InitFL(VAR FL : File;                      (* file defin. *)
                 FLName : ARRAY OF CHAR);            (* file name *)
BEGIN
  Lookup(FL,                         (* look up file on disk *)
         FLName,
         FALSE);
  IF (FL.res = done) THEN            (* error? *)
    SetModify(FL);                   (* set file for modify *)
  END;    (* IF *)
END InitFL;

(* Read description from file for specified crew member *)
PROCEDURE ReadDes(VAR FL : File;            (* file defin. *)
                  CrNum : CARDINAL;         (* crew mem num *)
                  VAR Des : ARRAY OF CHAR);   (* job des. *)
VAR
  i : CARDINAL;                (* array index *)
  ch : CHAR;                   (* holds character *)
BEGIN                          (* set file position *)
  SetPos(FL,                   (* file *)
         0,                    (* character position, high part *)
         (((CrNum-1)*LenCrData)+LenCrNum));   (* low part *)
  IF (FL.res = done) THEN      (* skip if error *)
    i := 0;
    REPEAT                     (* read description *)
      ReadChar(FL,             (* char by char *)
               ch);
      Des[i] := ch;            (* abort if error *)
      INC(i);
    UNTIL ((i > HIGH(Des)) OR (FL.res # done));
  END;    (* IF *)
```

```
END ReadDes;

(* Update description on file for specified crew member *)
PROCEDURE UpdtFL(VAR FL : File;            (* file defin. *)
                    CrNum : CARDINAL;      (* crew mem num *)
                    Des : ARRAY OF CHAR);  (* job des. *)
VAR
   i : CARDINAL;      (* array index *)
   ch : CHAR;         (* holds character *)
BEGIN                 (* set file position *)
   SetPos(FL,         (* file *)
          0,          (* character position, high part *)
          (((CrNum−1)*LenCrData)+LenCrNum));    (* low part *)
   IF (FL.res = done) THEN      (* skip if error *)
      i := 0;
      REPEAT                     (* write description *)
         ch := Des[i];          (* char by char *)
         WriteChar(FL,
                   ch);
         INC(i);
      UNTIL ((i > HIGH(Des)) OR (FL.res # done));
   END;      (* IF *)
END UpdtFL;

BEGIN                          (* main body *)
   WriteLn;
   WriteString("Start file update");

   InitFL(FL1,                 (* initialize first file *)
          "A:CREW1.TXT");      (* drive/file name *)
   InitFL(FL2,                 (* initialize second file *)
          "A:CREW2.TXT");      (* drive/file name *)
   IF ((FL1.res = done) AND (FL2.res = done)) THEN   (* error? *)
      LOOP                                            (* no *)
         WriteLn;
         WriteString("Enter crew number: ");
         ReadCard(CrewNum);
         IF (CrewNum = 0) THEN      (* crew num = 0? *)
            EXIT;                    (* yes—quit *)
         END;      (* IF *)

         ReadDes(FL1,CrewNum,JobDes);   (* read des. from file *)
         IF (FL1.res # done) THEN        (* error? *)
            EXIT;                        (* yes *)
```

```
    END;       (* IF *)

    WriteLn;
    WriteString("old job description: ");
    WriteString( JobDes);

    WriteLn;
    WriteString("enter new job description: ")
    ReadString( JobDes);

    UpdtFL(FL1,CrewNum,JobDes);      (* update des. on file 1 *)
    IF (FL1.res # done) THEN          (* error? *)
       EXIT;                          (* yes *)
    END;       (* IF *)

    UpdtFL(FL2,CrewNum,JobDes);      (* update des. on file 2 *)
    IF (FL2.res # done) THEN          (* error? *)
       EXIT;                          (* yes *)
    END;       (* IF *)

   END;       (* LOOP *)
 END;       (* IF done *)

IF (FL1.res = done) THEN        (* error on file? *)
   Close(FL1);                   (* no—close it *)
END;

IF (FL2.res = done) THEN        (* error on file? *)
   Close(FL2);                   (* no—close it *)
END;

IF ((FL1.res # done) OR (FL2.res # done)) THEN
   WriteLn;                               (* error encountered *)
   WriteString("error encountered while accessing file");
END;

WriteLn;
WriteString("End file update");
WriteLn;

END FileUpdt.
```

The program accepts a crew-member number from the keyboard, reads the job description from the file for that crew member, displays the job description, obtains a new description from the keyboard, and updates the description on the two files. An entry of 0 for the crew-member number terminates the program.

The program imports the usual procedures from InOut for interfacing with the terminal. Because no OpenInput or OpenOutput procedures are executed from InOut, the ReadCard, ReadString, WriteLn, and WriteString statements cause activity at the terminal instead of in a file.

Module Filesystem handles file access. A RECORD type, File, enumeration type, Response, and six procedures are imported from the module. Appendix B.5 lists the complete module interface.

A File variable contains status, definition, and bookkeeping information for a file. This information identifies the file to FileSystem procedures. The most important field within File is res, an enumeration that conveys the results of the last file operation. After accessing FileSystem procedure calls involving I/O, the program tests res for done to verify successful completion of the operation.

To demonstrate the multifile-access mechanism of FileSystem, the program issues the same updates to two identical files. FileSystem can deal with each file individually because the variable name is prefixed to all file references. Consequently, several files may be accessed concurrently. The actual number of files is limited only by memory and operating-system considerations.

File processing begins with the call to local procedure InitFL, which in turn calls the FileSystem procedure Lookup. The heading of this procedure is

```
PROCEDURE Lookup(VAR f : File;
                 Filename : ARRAY OF CHAR;
                 new : BOOLEAN);
```

Lookup searches the disk for the specified file name. If it exists, it is opened under variable f. If it does not exist and new is TRUE, it is created. The result field indicates the outcome:

f.res = done   if file exists or is created
f.res = notdone   if file does not exist and new = FALSE

If f.res does not equal done or notdone, an error occurred. Enumeration values done and notdone are part of type Response.

The program FileUpdt assmes that the files already exist, so FALSE is passed as the new parameter.

The next call in the InitFL procedure invokes procedure SetModify of the FileSystem module. SetModify sets the file state for modification, allowing both reading and writing.

Back in the main body of the program, the second file is initialized the same way. Before continuing with the main loop, the program interrogates the file-result field for done to ensure that no disk errors interfered with the successful completion of the Lookup operations. Throughout the program, the result is checked after FileSystem calls involving I/O. If it indicates an error condition, the program is aborted and the message "error encountered while accessing file" is displayed.

File Position

With module FileSystem, file access occurs relative to a file position. The position indicates the character (or characters) to be processed by the next read or write. Because the file of crew-member information is updated relative to the crew number, program FileUpdt calculates the file position for a crew-member entry.

When the file was created, each entry contained 36 characters. Thus, to access the first entry, the program would position itself at character 0; the second entry is at character 36; the fifth, at character 114; the eighth, at character 252, and so on.

The LOOP section of the program issues the actual read and write operations. Local procedure ReadDes finds the job description on file for a crew-member. It accomplishes this through the FileSystem procedures SetPos and ReadChar. SetPos sets the character position of the file for subsequent reading or writing. It accepts parameters in the form

```
PROCEDURE SetPos(VAR f : File;
                 highpos,
                 lowpos : CARDINAL);
```

The file position is set to

$$(highpos * (2^{16})) + lowpos$$

The position is relative to 0. To position to the first character of the file, the call

```
SetPos(f,0,0);
```

would be issued.

The file position is expressed with two CARDINAL variables, so that positions greater than or equal to 65,536 may be accessed. For example, to set the file-character position to 70,000, the expression

```
SetPos(f,1,4464);
```

could be written. Observe that

$$70000 - 65536 = 4464$$

Following SetPos, the program reads the job description character by character with the ReadChar procedure. ReadChar reads the character at the current file position and increments the position by 1.

The description is displayed and a new description is accepted from the terminal keyboard; that new description is then written on the file. Before the description is written, the file position must be reset because the preceding calls to ReadChar left it pointing to the character following the job description.

Program FileUpdt summarizes module FileSystem in a nutshell. Depending on the application, it might be desirable to expand on the error reporting and indicate the specific condition causing the error. Appendix B.5 shows the other values besides done that may be assigned to res, the result field.

5.6 *Type* POINTER

Variables of types ARRAY and RECORD remain fixed in size throughout their existence. RECORD variants do include additional flexibility, but overall, the dimensions of these structures must be known before they can be declared. In many cases, however, the data managed by a program grows and shrinks during execution. Must maximum-size structures be allocated, hogging acres of memory, to accommodate all possible cases?

The answer is no if the data structure is constructed with POINTER types, which are the building blocks of *dynamic data structures.* Dynamic data structures expand and contract like an accordion. They can be collapsed to nothing or expanded continually until the memory capacity of the computer is exhausted. Widely varying lists, such as compiler cross-reference tables, recursion stacks, and simulation queues, often fit the loose mold of dynamic data structures.

A simple example is the problem of sorting the ages of a ship's crew members. In an earlier chapter this was accomplished by setting up an array for 25 crew members, accepting the ages from the keyboard, and sorting them using a bubble-sort algorithm.

To make this program more general, the array can be replaced with a dynamically allocated *linked list.* POINTER variables connect the elements, or *nodes,* of the list. With this type of structure, the crew-member ages of any size ship can be accommodated. Furthermore, the ages are maintained in sequence, eliminating the need for a separate sort step. Program 5–4 demonstrates the use of pointers in this capacity.

Program 5–4 SortAgePntr

```
MODULE SortAgePntr;    (* Build sorted age list using pointers *)

FROM InOut IMPORT WriteLn,
                  WriteString,
                  WriteCard,
                  ReadCard;

FROM Storage IMPORT ALLOCATE;    (* NEW is automatically
                                    translated to
                                    ALLOCATE *)

TYPE
   AgePntr = POINTER TO AgeNode;
   AgeNode =           (* list entry, age/next pointer *)
     RECORD
       CrewMemAge : CARDINAL;
       NextAge : AgePntr;
     END;

VAR
   YoungPntr,          (* list pointers: youngest age *)
   NewPntr,            (*                new age entry *)
   CurrPntr,           (*                current one for search *)
   PrevPntr : AgePntr; (*                previous one for search *)
```

```
BEGIN
  YoungPntr := NIL;        (* initially set list null *)
  WriteLn;
  WriteString("Enter crew ages: ");
  WriteLn;

  LOOP
    NEW(NewPntr);          (* allocate space for list entry *)
    WriteLn;
    ReadCard(NewPntr ↑ .CrewMemAge);      (* accept age from
                                              keyboard *)
    IF (NewPntr ↑ .CrewMemAge = 0) THEN      (* age = 0? *)
      EXIT;                (* yes—input done *)
    END;     (* IF *)     (* no—add age in list by ascending order *)
    PrevPntr := NIL;              (* set previous pointer to NIL *)
    CurrPntr := YoungPntr;        (* set current pointer to youngest *)

    (* find place in list where age belongs *)
    WHILE ((CurrPntr # NIL) AND
            (NewPntr ↑ .CrewMemAge > CurrPntr ↑ .CrewMemAge))
          DO
      PrevPntr := CurrPntr;
      CurrPntr := CurrPntr ↑ .NextAge;
    END;     (* WHILE *)      (* quit searching if end of list or new
                                  age <= current age on list *)

    IF (CurrPntr # NIL) THEN      (* new age <= current age on
                                      list? *)
      NewPntr ↑ .NextAge := CurrPntr;    (* yes—put new in
                                              front *)
    ELSE
      NewPntr ↑ .NextAge := NIL;    (* no—put new at end *)
    END;     (* IF *)

    IF (PrevPntr # NIL) THEN      (* is new before youngest or is
                                      list null? *)
      PrevPntr ↑ .NextAge := NewPntr;      (* no—point previous at
                                                new *)
    ELSE
      YoungPntr := NewPntr;       (* yes—point youngest at new *)
    END;     (* IF *)

  END;     (* LOOP *)                         (* get next age *)

  WriteLn;
```

```
WriteString("Sorted ages:");
WriteLn;

CurrPntr := YoungPntr;              (* display ages in order *)
WHILE (CurrPntr # NIL) DO           (* end of list? *)
   WriteLn;                         (* no *)
   WriteCard(CurrPntr ↑ .CrewMemAge,0);
   CurrPntr := CurrPntr ↑ .NextAge;    (* point to next one *)
END;      (* WHILE *)

END SortAgePntr.
```

In this program, the statement

```
AgePntr = POINTER TO AgeNode;
```

defines AgePntr as a pointer to variables of type AgeNode. In the VAR section of the program, four pointer variables of this type are declared.

Only the operations of assignment and *dereferencing* and the relational operators equal (=) and not equal (#) apply to type POINTER. In assignments, POINTER variables are compatible with variables of the exact same type. For example, given the declarations

```
TYPE
   p1 = POINTER TO t1;
   p2 = POINTER TO t2;
 . . .
VAR
   pntr1 : p1;
   pntr2 : p2;
```

the assignment

```
pntr1 := pntr2;
```

is *illegal* because t1 and t2 are dissimilar types.

The up-arrow, or *dereferencing operator*, as shown in the program SortAgePntr, signifies the object referenced by a pointer. Specifically, NewPntr ↑ .CrewMemAge references the CrewMemAge variable to which the value in NewPntr points.

NIL *Pointer*

The reserved word NIL indicates a null pointer value. The expression

```
IF (CurrPntr # NIL) ...
```

is analogous to saying, "if CurrPntr is not NIL"—in other words, "if CurrPntr is pointing to something." In program SortAgePntr, as in many applications of linked lists, a NIL pointer value indicates the end of the list.

When working with pointers, you need not have a knowledge of the internal representation of the pointer variable. It suffices to know that a pointer is equal or not equal to another pointer or NIL, as shown in the program SortAgePntr. The relational operators "=" and "#" appear only with pointers in statements such as

```
IF (NewPntr = CurrPntr) . . .
IF (PrevPntr # NIL) . . .
```

Statements of the form

```
IF (NewPntr = Ø) . . .
IF (PrevPntr < CurrPntr) . . .
```

are meaningless and *illegal*.

In keeping with the dynamic aspect of the linked list AgeNode in program SortAgePntr, no variables exist until they are explicitly created. The standard library procedure NEW performs the creation task. Specifically, the statement NEW(NewPntr) creates a data component of the type associated with NewPntr—in this case, AgeNode. NEW then sets the actual parameter, NewPntr, to point to the data. In other words, NewPntr receives the address of the data.

Procedure NEW

Calls to procedure NEW may also include RECORD variants. Specifically, NEW(p,t1,t2,...) creates a variable of the type associated with pointer p for tag fields t1, t2, and so on. If the tag constants are missing or only partially specified, the remaining variant with the maximum size is created.

For example, assume that types BOOLEAN and CARDINAL occupy one storage unit each and type REAL occupies two storage units. Then, given the RECORD variant defined in section 5.4, namely,

```
TYPE
  engine =
    RECORD
      CASE SmallCraft : BOOLEAN OF      (* 1 storage unit *)
          TRUE : SizeCC : CARDINAL; |    (* 1 storage unit *)
          FALSE : SizeLiter : REAL;      (* 2 storage units *)
      END;    (* CASE *)
    END;    (* RECORD *)
```

the statements

```
VAR
    enginepnt : POINTER TO engine;
    . . .
BEGIN
    NEW(enginepnt,TRUE);
```

create a record consisting of two fields, SmallCraft and SizeCC, totalling two storage units.

Similarly, the statement

```
NEW(enginepnt,FALSE);
```

creates a record consisting of two fields, SmallCraft and SizeLiter, totalling three storage units.

A call to procedure NEW without tag constants specifies the maximum size record. That is,

```
NEW(enginepnt);
```

allocates a record of three storage units.

Procedure NEW, although a library module, does not appear in the import list for program SortAgePntr. Modula-2 actually translates NEW procedure calls to ALLOCATE as follows:

```
NEW(p,t1,t2,...)
```

becomes

```
ALLOCATE(p,TSIZE(T,t1,t2,...));
```

where p is declared as VAR p : POINTER TO T; and t1,t2, ... are tag-field values. TSIZE(T) is a standard function procedure that returns the number of storage units assigned to a variable of type T. ALLOCATE resides in the standard library module Storage. This automatic translation explains why ALLOCATE is imported from Storage in the module heading of program SortAgePntr.

Figures 5–2 through 5–7 demonstrate the construction of the linked data in program SortAgePntr, by graphically depicting the evolution of the list, assuming that five ages—21, 19, 42, 32, and 32—are entered at the keyboard. Initially, the list is set null by the leading statement of the module body, YoungPntr := NIL; (see Figure 5–2). Next, the first age is entered at the keyboard and placed in the list (Figure 5–3). A younger age is then entered, necessitating adjustment of the list beginning (Figure 5–4). The third age is appended at the end (Figure 5–5), and the next age is inserted between the nodes for ages 21 and 42 (Figure 5–6). Finally, the last age goes after the node for age 21 (Figure 5–7).

YoungPntr

Figure 5–2 First Phase of the Construction of the Linked Data in Program SortAgePntr

YoungPntr

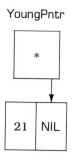

Figure 5–3 Second Phase of the Construction of the Linked Data in Program SortAgePntr

YoungPntr

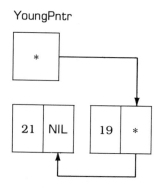

Figure 5–4 Third Phase of the Construction of the Linked Data in Program SortAgePntr

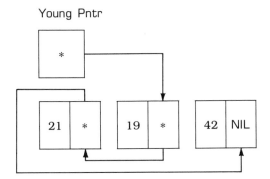

Figure 5–5 Fourth Phase of the Construction of the Linked Data in Program SortAgePntr

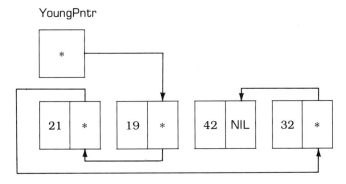

Figure 5–6 Fifth Phase of the Construction of the Linked Data in Program SortAgePntr

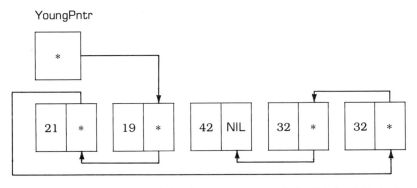

Figure 5–7 Sixth Phase of the Construction of the Linked Data in Program SortAgePntr

Creation of the list ends when an age of zero is entered. The WHILE loop in the last section of the module body then displays the ages in sorted order, namely, 19, 21, 32, 32, 42.

POINTER types adhere to the general, systematic syntax of Modula-2 in that they may be nested. After the five ages just mentioned have been entered in the linked list, the expressions

```
YoungPntr ↑ .NextAge ↑ .CrewMemAge
YoungPntr ↑ .NextAge ↑ .NextAge ↑ .CrewMemAge
YoungPntr ↑ .NextAge ↑ .NextAge ↑ .NextAge ↑ .CrewMemAge
```

refer to the second (age 21), third (age 32), and fourth (age 32) entries in the list.

Likewise,

```
IF (YoungPntr ↑ .NextAge = NIL) . . .
```

and

```
YoungPntr ↑ .NextAge ↑ .NextAge := CurrPntr;
```

are valid expressions.

Procedure DISPOSE

The algorithm in program SortAgePntr spawned a dynamic data structure from an initial null state, using procedure NEW. As mentioned earlier, though, pointer structures can be compacted as well as expanded. Compaction is handled by the standard procedure DISPOSE, which releases storage space allocated to a pointer variable.

DISPOSE resembles the format of NEW. It is automatically translated to the Storage module procedure DEALLOCATE as follows:

```
DISPOSE(p)
```

becomes

```
DEALLOCATE(p,TSIZE(T));
```

and

```
DISPOSE(p,t1,t2,...)
```

becomes

```
DEALLOCATE(p,TSIZE(T,t1,t2,...));
```

DISPOSE also sets p to NIL.

Besides NEW and DISPOSE, Storage provides another procedure, called Available, to help manage dynamic variables. Available determines if there is sufficient storage space to accommodate a variable of given size. The procedure is declared as

PROCEDURE Available(size : CARDINAL) : BOOLEAN;

It returns TRUE if there is space available to accommodate the number of bytes specified in the variable named size.

The following five rules summarize the use of pointers:

1. Every pointer is bound to a type. Its values point only to variables of that type.

2. Referenced variables can be accessed only by pointers.

3. Referenced variables are dynamically created by the statement NEW(p), which allocates storage space to the variable and assigns the variable's pointer to p. Similarly, DISPOSE(p) releases the storage space and assigns NIL to p.

4. The pointer constant NIL applies to every pointer type and points to no object.

5. The designator p ↑ references the variable pointed to by p. If p is NIL, the designator p ↑ is undefined.

5.7 *Type* PROCEDURE

The reserved word PROCEDURE in Modula-2 resembles the words *bat* and *lie* in the English language. Bat can mean either flying mammal or club, and lie can mean either recline or prevaricate, depending on the surrounding prose. Similarly, the word PROCEDURE can either indicate a group of instructions in a module or appear as the type declaration of a variable.

PROCEDURE-type variables provide a method of referring to procedures through additional names. They can also pass procedure identifiers to parameters in procedure headings.

Consider the statements

```
TYPE
   DispProc = PROCEDURE(CARDINAL,
                        CARDINAL);
VAR
   outp : DispProc;
```

which declare a procedure variable containing two formal CARDINAL parameters. The definition outlined in the TYPE declaration controls the kinds of procedures that may be assigned to the procedure variable.

For example, WriteCard could be assigned to outp, because WriteCard has two CARDINAL parameters. Its actual definition is

```
PROCEDURE WriteCard(x,
                    n : CARDINAL);
```

After the assignment

```
outp := WriteCard;
```

outp will mimic WriteCard. Specifically,

```
outp(c,5);
```

produces the same result as

```
WriteCard(c,5);
```

The cardinal display procedure can still be invoked through WriteCard; outp simply becomes another alias for it.

If the procedure type has no parameters, its declaration can be abbreviated using the standard type PROC. PROC is formally defined as

```
TYPE
  PROC = PROCEDURE;
```

An application of PROC would be

```
VAR
  WLn : PROC;
. . .
  WLn := WriteLn;    (* WriteLn has no parameters *)
```

Procedure types can also be declared as functions of the form

```
TYPE
  TrigFunc = PROCEDURE(REAL) : REAL;
VAR
  calcp : TrigFunc;

  . . .

  calcp := sin;
```

If the function procedure type lacks parameters, an empty list must be included, as it is with function procedure declarations:

```
TYPE
  StatFunc = PROCEDURE( ) : INTEGER;
VAR
  DoStat : StatFunc;
  i : INTEGER;

  . . .

  i := DoStat( );
```

Program 5–5 demonstrates an application of procedure type variables by selecting alternate modes of display. The program accepts a cardinal decimal value from the keyboard and displays its octal or hexadecimal equivalent, according to the operator's selection.

Program 5–5 ConvertDec

```
MODULE ConvertDec;      (* Convert decimal number to octal or hex
                           using procedure variables *)

FROM InOut IMPORT WriteLn,
                  WriteOct,
                  WriteHex,
                  WriteString,
                  ReadCard,
                  Read;

TYPE
  DispProc = PROCEDURE(CARDINAL,
                       CARDINAL);

VAR
  outp : DispProc;        (* procedure variable *)
  InNum : CARDINAL;
  ch : CHAR;
```

```
PROCEDURE ShowAnswer(showproc : DispProc;
                          number : CARDINAL);

BEGIN
  WriteLn;
  WriteString("Converted result = ");
  showproc(number,Ø);
  WriteLn;
END ShowAnswer;

BEGIN
  WriteLn;
  WriteString("Enter value to be converted: ");
  ReadCard(InNum);
  WriteLn;
  WriteString("Convert to hex? ");
  Read(ch);
  IF (CAP(ch) = "Y") THEN        (* convert to hex? *)
    outp := WriteHex;            (* yes—use hex procedure *)
  ELSE
    outp := WriteOct;            (* no—assume octal *)
  END;      (* IF *)
  ShowAnswer(outp,InNum);

END ConvertDec.
```

5.8 Summary/Problems

PROCEDURE types allow procedures to be handled as variables. They can be passed as parameters and accessed through multiple identifiers. Effectively, alternate procedures can be selected during the course of a program's execution by assigning different values to procedure variables. Although infrequently used, they do add another degree of flexibility to the programming environment.

POINTER types, on the other hand, are enlisted for active duty fairly often, in particular as the framework for dynamic data structures. During execution, dynamic structures grow and shrink like a balloon, based on the storage requirements of the data.

Practically speaking, pointers reference only variables of type RECORD because the pointer to the next element can be included in the record data structure. RECORD types, like ARRAY types, are composed of component parts. Although an ARRAY must consist of elements of the same type, RECORDs can embody dissimilar elements. Furthermore, RECORD variants effectively infuse the structure with the quick-change artistry of a chameleon, allowing it to change its form depending on the value of the tag field. Variables of type RECORD commonly contain file data and linked structures.

The other topics covered in this chapter spell out disk file management. Standard module InOut sequentially processes at most one input file and one output file. It also doubles as the standard terminal screen and keyboard interface and has been enlisted in this capacity since chapter 1.

Random file processing falls into the bailiwick of module FileSystem. Although FileSystem is an optional module, most systems include it because it was implemented as part of the original Modula-2 found on the Lilith.

Last but not least, recursion made its debut. Constructing recursive procedures in Modula-2 requires no special formatting—theoretically, any procedure can call itself. Often, the major decision regarding recursion is whether a recursive procedure should be substituted for an equivalent iterative scheme.

Problems

1. [M] Write a program to calculate the Fibonacci number n using a recursive procedure. The Fibonacci number is defined by the equations

   $Fib(1) = 1$
   $Fib(2) = 1$
   $Fib(n) = Fib(n-1) + Fib(n-2)$ if $n > 2$

2. [M] Write a program that sequentially reads the crew-member information in the file created by program FileMake, displays the information for each crew member on the screen, accepts a 20-character name from the keyboard, and writes the crew-member information along with the name to a new file. Each entry in the new file will consist of

characters 1–8   = crew-member number
characters 9–28   = crew-member name
characters 29–44 = job description

3. [M] Modify program SortAgePntr to maintain the ages in a *doubly linked list* so that an age node points to its successor as well as to its precedessor. Then display the sorted ages in descending as well as ascending order.

4. [M] Write a RECORD variant that stores the dimensions of a figure in fields of type REAL. Specifically, if the figure is a rectangle, it stores the height and width; if it is a square, it stores the length of one side; and if it is a circle, it stores the radius.

Figure 5–8 Reading data from external devices can sometimes be a trying experience.

6
Expert-level Seafaring

6. Expert-level Seafaring

The preceding chapters described the fundamental nautical tools of Modula-2. With these tools you can handily circumnavigate the computing sea. Still, there are those connoisseurs who remain restless without total mastery of the language. These are the skippers who hike sailboats out to 45 degree leans, traverse the Arctic in ice breakers, and float the Amazon to its headwaters. To accomplish feats out of the ordinary in Modula-2, you must notch your helm with instruction in expert-level seafaring before leaving port.

Certification in expert-level seafaring requires mastery of only three additional, albeit fairly formidable, principles:

1. Low-level facilities

2. Modules, including definition and implementation parts, export and import lists, and execution-time binding

3. Coroutines

Low-level facilities unveil the underlying software and hardware of computer systems, the raw character of the machine. Assembler-like operations can be performed within the scope of Modula-2's elegance and structure.

Modules have encapsulated this book's programs since the first chapter. Besides delineating the extent of a program, however, the MODULE structure can define precise protocol between independently developed parts of a large, multisegmented program. Modula-2 strictly enforces interface compatibility between modules, ensuring that individual components communicate on the same wave length. The role played by modules cannot be underestimated. According to Niklaus Wirth, "Modules are the most important feature distinguishing Modula-2 from its ancestor, Pascal."

A discussion of *coroutines* rounds out the chapter. Coroutines manage execution of concurrent processes. They are designed to handle the spontaneous, unpredictable activity of hardware interrupt drivers, process schedulers, and other timesharing operations.

6.1 Low-level Facilities

One of the hallmarks of a high-level language is that the programmer is insulated from the intricacies of the hardware. Essentially, programs can be written without worrying about the idiosyncrasies of the underlying machinery.

Still, there are situations in which it is not only desirable but necessary to dip into the deepest recesses of the hardware. Device drivers, communications handlers, and memory mapped input and output are a few of the applications that defy expression in most high-level languages.

To operate at the lowest levels of the hardware, Modula-2 provides *low-level facilities*, which divide into three categories:

1. *Type-transfer functions* that circumvent the usual, rigorous type checking

2. Declaration of variables at *absolute memory locations*

3. Types and procedures of module SYSTEM for determining the machine-level representation of variables and manipulating data at the machine level

Type-Transfer Functions

Type-transfer functions offer the flexibility of bypassing Modula-2's rigorous type checking. They transfer variable contents regardless of declared types, which facilitates machine-level manipulation of data. Along with the easing of type rules, however, comes less protection from programming errors and reduced portability of programs, because the internal representations of data are usually machine-dependent.

Type-transfer functions essentially convert variables from one type to another. The functions are expressed by writing the type name with the variable. For example,

```
VAR
  b : BOOLEAN;
  ch : CHAR;
. . .
  b := BOOLEAN(ch);
```

assigns to the BOOLEAN variable b the contents of CHAR variable ch.

Type-transfer functions *do not* involve any actual computations—they merely relax type checking and transfer the internal representation of a variable. Knowledge of the internal format of variables on the host computer is required to use these functions effectively. The type associated with the function merely indicates the intended interpretation of the result.

Other examples of type transfer functions are

```
TYPE
  scales = ARRAY[1..25] OF CARDINAL;
  measures =
    RECORD
      temp : [-50..130];
      speed : [0..55];
      misc : ARRAY[1..23] OF INTEGER;
    END;
VAR
  sc : scales;
  ms : measures;
  i : INTEGER;
  c : CARDINAL;
. . .
  ms := measures(sc);
  i := i + INTEGER(c);
```

These examples highlight the main restriction of type-transfer functions—the machine-level representations of each of the variables in an expression with a type-transfer function must occupy the same amount of memory storage. In this case, the assumption is made that CARDINAL and INTEGER variables occupy the same amount of storage. This assumption holds on most Modula-2 systems.

Overall, type-transfer functions should be reserved for those situations in which Modula-2's standard, more respectable type-transfer functions, ORD, CHR, and VAL, prove unsuitable.

Absolute Memory Locations

The second low-level facility, declaring variables at absolute memory locations, has particular application in *memory-mapped* computer systems. These systems typically reserve certain locations in memory for items such as the screen buffer, interrupt vectors, and file-control blocks.

To place a variable at a specific location, include the location in brackets after the identifier name. For example,

```
VAR
  EndMemory[65535] : CARDINAL;
  ResetPntr[0FFFEH] : INTEGER;
  NMIPntr[0FFFCH] : INTEGER;
```

declares three variables at memory locations decimal 65535, hexadecimal 0FFFEH and hexadecimal 0FFFCH. The *H* appended to the number signifies a hexadecimal value.

SYSTEM *Types*

The third category of low-level facilities is made up of the types and procedures of module SYSTEM. SYSTEM has the properties of a library module, except that it is integral to the compiler. SYSTEM still has to be imported, but it does not actually reside in an external module library. Consequently, it is called a *pseudomodule*.

SYSTEM contains the types WORD and ADDRESS. WORD is generally used in procedures that operate on arguments of different types. Formal procedure parameters of type WORD are type-compatible with any actual parameter that occupies one word of storage. The size of a storage word depends on the implementation. On 16-bit computer systems, a word typically occupies 16 bits.

The only operator that applies to WORD variables is assignment, and

WORD variables are incompatible with all other types, with the exception of parameter lists. Of course, type-transfer functions may be called upon to defeat these limitations.

The incompatibility limitation does not apply to open array parameters of base type WORD. Open arrays of WORD are compatible with all types, including RECORDs and SETs. As a result, any variable can be interpreted as an array of words.

The following program segment illustrates the generality of type WORD. The function procedure Sum totals either an integer or cardinal array, producing an integer result.

```
FROM SYSTEM IMPORT WORD;
VAR
   ac : ARRAY[1..5] OF CARDINAL;
   ai : ARRAY[1..5] OF INTEGER;

. . .
PROCEDURE Sum(a : ARRAY OF WORD) : INTEGER;
  VAR
    j : CARDINAL;
    total : INTEGER;
  BEGIN
    total := 0;
    FOR j := 0 TO HIGH(a) BY 1 DO
       INC(total,INTEGER(a[j]));     (* use INTEGER type *)
    END;     (* FOR *)               (* transfer function *)
    RETURN total;
  END Sum;

. . .
   Sum(ac);     (* call Sum with cardinal argument *)
   Sum(ai);     (* call Sum with integer argument *)
```

In the INC statement, the type-transfer function INTEGER(a[j]) tells the compiler to treat the WORD variable, a[j], as an integer. Although this scheme lends a degree of flexibility to the summation procedure, the programmer must ensure that cardinal array elements will not exceed the range of integer variables; otherwise, the results will be unpredictable.

Accompanying type WORD in the module SYSTEM is ADDRESS, which is defined as

```
TYPE
   ADDRESS = POINTER TO WORD;
```

ADDRESS denotes CARDINAL-compatible pointer variables that may be used in arithmetic operations.

SYSTEM *Procedures*

For data manipulation, module SYSTEM hosts three function procedures, named ADR, SIZE, and TSIZE. Each of these procedures accepts one parameter of any type.

ADR(x) returns the memory location of variable x. The returned value is of type ADDRESS.

SIZE(x) returns the number of storage units assigned to variable x. The returned value is of type CARDINAL. If the parameter x contains a RECORD variant, the maximum possible record size is returned. SIZE does not accept open arrays.

TSIZE(t) returns the number of storage units assigned to type t. The returned value is of type CARDINAL. TSIZE works as SIZE does on RECORD variants, with one minor twist. Tag field constants may be optionally specified to select a particular variant. If the tag constants are missing or only partially specified, the remaining variant with the maximum size is returned.

For example, given the following declaration of record type engine, cited previously:

```
TYPE
  engine =
    RECORD
        CASE SmallCraft : BOOLEAN OF       (* 1 storage unit *)
            TRUE : SizeCC : CARDINAL; |     (* 1 storage unit *)
            FALSE : SizeLiter : REAL;        (* 2 storage units *)
        END;      (* CASE *)
    END;      (* RECORD *)
```

the following procedure calls yield the results indicated:

```
TSIZE(engine);              (* yields 3 *)
TSIZE(engine,TRUE);         (* yields 2 *)
TSIZE(engine,FALSE);        (* yields 3 *)
```

The storage units returned by SIZE and TSIZE are usually expressed in bytes. The actual size of a storage unit should be described precisely in the system-dependencies section of the compiler documentation.

6.2 *Local* MODULEs

It is somewhat ironic that although the MODULE statement appears at the beginning of every program that has been discussed so far, it has not received comprehensive treatment until now. This is because of the wide-ranging complexity of modules. In unadorned form, they simply encapsulate a group of related procedures and data. Fully decked, however, modules serve as the brick and mortar of sophisticated software architecture. They cleanly conceal local data elements from the global spectrum, preserving data integrity; they embody library procedures, saving programmers from having to reinvent the wheel; and they spell out and enforce very exact interfaces, allowing distinct parts of multifaceted programs to be developed simultaneously.

These concepts will be illustrated by taking a common computing problem—generation of random numbers—and implementing it as a MODULE. The solution employs the mixed congruential random number algorithm. Initially, it accepts a random seed, say $x0$, and produces random number $x1$. The algorithm then accepts $x1$ to produce $x2$, $x2$ to produce $x3$, and so on. Program 6–1 implements the algorithm.

RandomNo is the main, top-level module in Program 6–1. It encompasses one local variable, i, and one *local module*, RandNum. RandNum is called local because it is declared within the main module instead of being imported from the module library.

The syntax of a local module resembles a procedure. It has its own body (designated by BEGIN/END), CONST, TYPE, VAR, and procedure declarations. Modules also contain *export and import lists*, which are missing from procedures.

Program 6–1 RandomNo

```
MODULE RandomNo;      (* Generate random numbers *)
FROM InOut IMPORT WriteCard,
                  WriteLn,
                  WriteString;

VAR
   i : CARDINAL;                              (* counter *)

  MODULE RandNum;
    EXPORT Random;
    VAR
      Seed : CARDINAL;
      SystemTime[046CH] : CARDINAL;      (* system time *)

    PROCEDURE Random( ) : CARDINAL;
    BEGIN      (* use mixed congruential formula *)
      Seed := (((Seed * 21) + 13) MOD 256);
      RETURN Seed;
    END Random;

  BEGIN      (* RandNum *)
    Seed := SystemTime;      (* set initial seed to time *)
  END RandNum;

BEGIN                       (* main module *)
  WriteLn;
  WriteString("Generate 256 random numers");
  WriteLn;

  FOR i := 1 TO 256 BY 1 DO
    WriteLn;
    WriteCard(Random( ),0);
  END;      (* FOR *)

END RandomNo.
```

Although procedures and modules resemble each other in syntax, major functional differences distinguish these two constructs. Of primary concern are their lifespans. Procedures exist only for the duration of a procedure call. After the procedure terminates, its identifiers, such as constants, variables, and local procedures, vanish. Module identifiers, on the other hand, remain active as long as the calling module is active.

The random-number program demonstrates this concept. Between calls to RandNum's local procedure Random, variable Seed maintains its value.

If Random were not surrounded by a module, it would be necessary for the calling program to pass the previous random number to Random so that the next random number could be generated.

One exception to the rule regarding the longevity of modules involves modules that are *local to a procedure*. These modules, like any other local identifier belonging to the procedure, expire when the procedure terminates. The following program segment illustrates a module that is local to a procedure.

```
MODULE MainMod;        (* main module *)
  PROCEDURE P1;        (* local procedure belonging to MainMod *)
    . . .
    MODULE Mod1;       (* local module belonging to P1, exists only when
                          P1 is active *)

    . . .
    END Mod1;
  END P1;
  BEGIN       (* MainMod *)
    . . .
    P1;

  . . .
  END MainMod.
```

The only objects visible outside of the module RandNum are those named in the export list, designated by the statement EXPORT. In this case, that includes only one object, the function procedure Random. The specifics of the random-number generator—the seed and formula—remain hidden in the module.

RandNum contains two executable parts: the function procedure Random and the module body. As you may have guessed, the procedure is executed like any other procedure, namely, through a call statement in the main module. The module body, which contains one instruction, is executed *automatically* before the first call to the local procedure is made. Execution of the module body occurs only once.

Module bodies are optional; where they are needed, however, their benefits are indispensable. They remove the burden of initialization housekeeping from the main body and place it in the corresponding procedure. The intricate details of data structure and logic remain within the confines of the procedure rather than floating to the top level of the program.

Besides being placed within other modules, as just illustrated, local modules can be placed within procedures.

The only assumption that can be made about the actual execution sequence of module bodies is that module bodies are executed *before* the module is called. No assumptions can be made about the *actual execution sequence* of multiple module bodies.

The visibility of module identifiers (such as module constants, variables, and procedures) is controlled by *import* and *export* lists. Program 6–2 illustrates the sharing of identifiers between modules through these lists. This program displays

```
Start Main
Processing DoThreeMod
Z
Finish Main
```

Program 6–2 ModDemo

```
MODULE ModDemo;      (* Show execution of module bodies *)

FROM InOut IMPORT Write
                  WriteLn,
                  WriteString;

VAR
  a : INTEGER;

PROCEDURE DoThreeMod;

  MODULE M1;
    IMPORT e;
    EXPORT b,
            c;
    VAR
      b : CARDINAL;

    MODULE M2;
      IMPORT b;
      EXPORT c;
      VAR
        c : CHAR;
    BEGIN     (* M2 *)      (* b, c visible here *)
      b := 0;
      c := "X";
    END M2;

  BEGIN     (* M1 *)      (* b, c, e visible here *)
    b := 0;
    c := "Y";
```

```
    e := 1.2;
  END M1;
  MODULE M3;
    IMPORT a;
    EXPORT QUALIFIED b;
    VAR
      b,
      d : REAL;
  BEGIN     (* M3 *)        (* a, M3.b, d visible here *)
    a := -1;
    b := 3.4;
    d := 5.6;
  END M3;

VAR
  e : REAL;                 (* local to procedure *)

BEGIN     (* DoThreeMod *)     (* a, b, M3.b, c, e visible
                                  here *)

  a := -1;
  b := 0;                   (* unqualified refers to M1's *)
  M1.b := 0;                (* optionally qualified reference *)
  M3.b := 7.8;              (* mandatory qualified reference *)
  c := "Z";                 (* procedure assignments *)
  e := 0.0;                 (* supersede module bodies *)
  WriteLn;
  WriteString("Processing DoThreeMod");
  WriteLn;
  Write(c);
END DoThreeMod;

BEGIN     (* ModDemo *)     (* only a visible here *)
  WriteLn;
  WriteString("Start Main");
  WriteLn;

  DoThreeMod;

  a := -9;

  WriteLn;
  WriteString("Finish Main");
  WriteLn;

END ModDemo.
```

The three rules governing module *scope of visibility* are

1. The visibility range of a module identifier can be extended by listing it in the module's *export list*.

2. The exported identifiers of a local module are not visible to another local module unless they are included in the latter's *import list*. All exported identifiers are visible to the local procedure.

3. Only the main module can import identifiers directly from an external module.

When an identifier crosses several module boundries, such as when variable c goes from M2 to M1 to the procedure DoThreeMod, the identifier must be listed in the respective export lists. The local variables of ModDemo and DoThreeMod, a and e, are visible only to the modules that import them.

Qualified References

The identifier b presents a dilemma because it is exported from modules M1 and M3 at the same level. To prevent ambiguity, the export is *qualified* in M3. M3's exported item is referred through a *qualified identifier*. The syntax of qualified identifiers is identical to field selectors of RECORD types.

If the reserved word EXPORT is followed by the symbol QUALIFIED, the listed identifiers must be prefixed with the module's identifier when used outside the module.

Qualified references of the form M3.b access the variable b defined in module M3. Unqualified references of the form b, or optionally qualified references of the form M1.b, access the variable with respect to M1. Qualified identifiers cannot appear in import or export lists.

In practice, few local modules employ qualified identifiers because the programmer has control over the assignment of identifiers and can easily choose names that do not clash. On the other hand, qualified identifiers are mandatory in *global modules*, in which assumptions cannot be made about the uniqueness of an identifier name. The concept of global modules will be introduced in the next section.

Another method of exporting identifiers is by exporting the entire module. Placing the module name in the export list causes all of its identifiers to be exported. Program 6–3 illustrates this kind of export.

The visibility of constant x passes through three modules as each module name is exported. At the level of the main module, the constant can simply be referred to as x. The references A.x, A.B.x, and A.B.C.x are optionally qualified to highlight the hierarchical nature of qualified identifiers. Essentially, qualified identifiers follow the same syntax as record

Program 6–3 Main

MODULE Main;

FROM InOut IMPORT Write;

MODULE A;
  EXPORT B;

                        (* x, B.x, C.x, B.C.x visible here *)

  MODULE B
    EXPORT C;

                        (* x, C.x visible here *)

    MODULE C
      EXPORT x;   (* x visible here *)
      CONST
        x = "!";
    END C;

  END B;

END A;

BEGIN   (* Main *)

  Write(x);   (* these all refer to x *)
  Write(A.x);
  Write(B.x);
  Write(C.x);
  Write(A.B.x);
  Write(A.C.x);
  Write(B.C.x);
  Write(A.B.C.x);

END Main.

variables containing field identifiers. The identifiers A.B.C.x could be described as identifier x belonging to module C, which belongs to module B, which belongs to module A.

A module name may also be imported, causing all identifiers of that module's export list to be imported. For example, in the program ModDemo, if the statement

IMPORT M1;

appeared in a module, it would import variables b and c. References to those variables would have to be made through qualified identifiers, M1.b and M1.c.

Unqualified References

Prefixing an import list with the reserved word FROM, followed by the module name, *unqualifies* the identifiers. This book's references to procedures in module InOut have all been made through unqualified identifiers of the form

```
FROM InOut IMPORT WriteLn,
                  WriteString;
. . .
WriteLn;
WriteString("Watching the ships roll in . . .");
```

If the entire module were imported, the procedure references would have to be qualified:

```
IMPORT InOut;
. . .
InOut.WriteLn;
InOut.WriteString("Watching the ships roll in . . .");
```

This method offers the opportunity to redefine unqualified references to WriteString. A local declaration of WriteString could be used to display with a special video effect, say highlighting. Simple calls of the form WriteString would go to the local procedure; access to the library procedure would require the qualified identifier InOut.WriteString.

With that said, most of the salient attributes of import and export lists have been covered. Only three points remain:

1. A module may have many import lists, but it can only have one export list.

2. Each import list may reference only one module. Statements of the form

```
IMPORT M1, M2;
```

are *illegal* and must be written as

```
IMPORT M1;
IMPORT M2;
```

3. If a RECORD or enumeration type is exported, all field identifiers or constant values are exported, too. For example,

```
MODULE FileSystem;               (* exporting module *)
EXPORT QUALIFIED File,           (* exports all fields *)
                 Response,       (* exports all identifiers *)
. . .
TYPE
  Response = (done, notdone, . . . );
  File =
    RECORD
        id : CARDINAL;
        eof : BOOLEAN;
        res : Response;
      . . .
  END Filesystem.
MODULE FileIO;      (* importing module *)
FROM FileSystem IMPORT File,     (* imports all fields *)
                  Response       (* done is implicitly
                                    imported as part of
                                    Response *)

. . .
VAR
  F1 : File;
. . .
  IF (F1.res = done) THEN
. . .
END FileIO.
```

6.3 MODULE DEFINITION *and* IMPLEMENTATION *Parts*

The previous discussion centered on local modules. Many modules, however, such as InOut, are external to the main calling program. These *global modules* are compiled separately and reside in the module library.

In general, most of the characteristics of local modules—module bodies, import/export lists, qualified/unqualified identifiers—also apply to separately compiled modules. The main distinction is that separately compiled modules may be split into two parts, a *definition part* and an *implementation part*. The definition part contains the declarations of the constants, types, variables, and procedure headings—in other words, all of the information needed to interface with the module. The *implementation part* completes the picture by supplying the actual statements that perform the module's action.

The primary benefit of dividing a module into definition and implementation parts is the separation, or *decoupling*, of interface data and operational details. The implementation part can be modified independently of the definition part, as long as the definition identifiers are not impacted. A data-retrieval algorithm, for example, could be changed from using a sequential search to using a binary search, leaving the definition part unchanged. Taking the random number generator and splitting it into implementation and definition parts will help illustrate the mechanics of separately compiled modules. The calling module of this generator would be:

```
MODULE RandomNo;      (* Generate random numbers, main calling
                            module *)
FROM InOut IMPORT WriteCard,
                  WriteLn,
                  WriteString;

FROM RandNum IMPORT Random;      (* Random procedure is
                                       external *)
VAR
  i : CARDINAL;      (* counter *)
BEGIN                (* main module *)
  WriteLn;
  WriteString("Generate 256 random numbers");
  WriteLn;
  FOR i := 1 TO 256 BY 1 DO
    WriteLn;
    WriteCard(Random( ),0);
  END;     (* FOR *)
END RandomNo.
```

The definition module for this program would be written as follows:

```
DEFINITION MODULE RandNum;
  EXPORT QUALIFIED Random;      (* export Random procedure *)
  PROCEDURE Random( ) : CARDINAL;      (* only procedure
                                           specification *)
END RandNum.      (* contained in definition module *)
```

The implementation module would be written as:

```
IMPLEMENTATION MODULE RandNum;
  VAR
    Seed : CARDINAL;
```

```
    SystemTime[046CH] : CARDINAL;        (* system time *)
    PROCEDURE Random() : CARDINAL;
    BEGIN     (* use mixed congruential formula *)
      Seed := (((Seed * 21) + 13) MOD 256);
      RETURN Seed;
    END Random;
  BEGIN      (* RandNum *)
    Seed := SystemTime;     (* set initial seed to time *)
  END RandNum.
```

This version of the random-number program consists of three *compilation units*: the calling module and the definition and implementation modules of the random-number generator. The definition module contains the constant, type, variable, and procedure heading declarations to be exported. Observe that the exported declarations (in this case, only procedure Random) appear in complete form in the implementation module. Furthermore, the identifiers Seed and SystemTime, because they are local, appear only in the implementation module.

Implementation modules encapsulate module declarations, procedure bodies, and module bodies. They may also contain import lists, but no export lists.

Definition modules, however, may contain both import and export lists. Import lists *must be* qualified with the reserved word FROM; they merely relay identifiers to the export lists. For example,

```
DEFINITION MODULE DoingIO;
  FROM InOut IMPORT EOL;
  EXPORT QUALIFIED EOL,
                   ScribbleOnDisk;
  PROCEDURE ScribbleOnDisk(s : ARRAY OF CHAR);
END DoingIO.
```

In this module, the constant EOL is imported for inclusion on the export list. It is *not* available to the implementation part of DoingIO. The implementation module would have to import it separately to use it.

The export list in a definition module is actually a redundant statement because Modula-2 automatically exports all identifiers that are declared in a definition module. Strictly speaking, the export list could be discarded. It is generally included, though, for explicit documentation.

As mentioned earlier, exporting a RECORD type or enumeration automatically exports the associated identifiers of the record fields or enumerated constants. This method of export is termed *transparent export*. In many situations, however, the programmer may want to mask the details of the data to prevent software from becoming unduly coupled with specific data structures. Modula-2 addresses this problem with a nontransparent kind of export entitled *opaque export.*

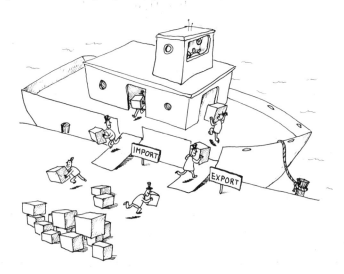

Opaque Export

Opaque export allows the name of a type identifier to be exported while the details of the type remain hidden. Because the type details are unknown, the importing module can manipulate variables of the opaque type only with procedures defined in the implementation module.

For example, consider a file-access module, a common application of opaque exports. As shown in the following program segments, the type identifier FileKey is declared in the definition module, but its details remain hidden in the implementation module in which it is fully defined.

```
MODULE FileProcess;     (* Importing module *)
FROM FileHandler IMPORT FileKey,
                        Open,
                        Read,
                        Close;
VAR
  InFile : FileKey;
BEGIN
  Open(InFile,"Dossier.txt");
```

```
...
END FileProcess.
```

```
DEFINITION MODULE FileHandler;
EXPORT QUALIFIED FileKey,
                 Open,
                 Read,
                 Close;
TYPE
   FileKey;      (* opaque type—since FileKey is unspecified in the
                    definition module, its structure is hidden from
                    importing modules *)
PROCEDURE Open(VAR f : FileKey;
                  name : ARRAY OF CHAR);

...
END FileHandler.
```

```
IMPLEMENTATION MODULE FileHandler;
TYPE
   FileKey = POINTER TO      (* opaque type defined here *)
                RECORD
                   Drive : CARDINAL;
                   eof : BOOLEAN;
                   BlockNum : CARDINAL;
                   NextByte : CARDINAL;
                END;
PROCEDURE Open(VAR f : FileKey;
                  name : ARRAY OF CHAR);

...
END FileHandler.
```

The only valid operations on variables of type FileKey are assignment, comparisons for equality and inequality, and parameter-passing to the procedures of the implementation module. Opaque exports are further restricted to POINTER types, as shown in the example with type FileKey.

The responsibility of verifying the validity of type interfaces between modules rests with the Modula-2 compiler and loader. During compilation, all interfaces are checked for validity of type identifiers between the importing and exporting modules. Conflicting interfaces result in the termination of the compilation with an appropriate error message.

When the program is loaded for execution, module interfaces are verified again. This second check ensures that the interface in a definition module was not modified subsequent to the compilation of the importing module. If the interface between the exporting and importing module conflicts, the program load is aborted and an error message is issued. Whenever a definition module is changed, all modules that import it should also be changed to avoid this type of error.

6.4 Coroutines

Because Modula-2 was designed to write operating systems, it includes *coroutines* for the expression of concurrent activities. *Coroutines* are procedures whose execution is triggered by an explicit transfer of control or by an event such as a hardware interrupt. A coroutine usually suspends its execution by transferring control to another procedure. Where the coroutine is reinvoked accounts for the primary difference between coroutines and procedures. Control returns to a coroutine at the instruction following the point of suspension. Procedures, on the other hand, always execute from the beginning.

There are three steps in setting up a procedure as a coroutine. First, the procedure heading and body is declared as usual for a procedure. Second, the procedure is designated as a *process* through the SYSTEM procedure NEWPROCESS; in Modula-2, *process* and *coroutine* are synonymous. Finally, control is passed to the coroutine through the SYSTEM procedure TRANSFER.

Program 6–4 relies on coroutines to display messages on the screen. Although this activity could be expressed easily without coroutines, the example demonstrates the mechanics of setting up coroutines and transferring control between them. The program continually displays on the terminal screen the message

DispProc1
DispProc2

Program 6–4 CoroutineDemo

```
MODULE CoroutineDemo;     (* display with coroutines *)

FROM InOut IMPORT WriteLn,
                  WriteString;

FROM SYSTEM IMPORT WORD,
                   PROCESS,
                   ADR,
                   SIZE,
                   NEWPROCESS,
                   TRANSFER;

VAR
  main,
  p1,
  p2 : PROCESS;             (* process variables *)
  wsp1,                     (* workspaces for processes *)
  wsp2 : ARRAY [1..100] OF WORD;

PROCEDURE DispProc1;
BEGIN
  LOOP
    WriteLn;
    WriteString("DispProc1");
    TRANSFER(p1,p2);        (* invoke other procedure *)
  END;     (* LOOP *)
END DispProc1;

PROCEDURE DispProc2;
BEGIN
  LOOP
    WriteLn;
    WriteString("DispProc2");
    TRANSFER(p2,p1);        (* invoke other procedure *)
  END;     (* LOOP *)
END DispProc2;

BEGIN     (* main module *)
  NEWPROCESS(DispProc1,
             ADR(wsp1),
             SIZE(wsp1),
             p1);
```

```
NEWPROCESS(DispProc2,
            ADR(wsp2),
            SIZE(wsp2),
            p2);
    TRANSFER(main,p1);

END CoroutineDemo.
```

The procedure NEWPROCESS of module SYSTEM creates the process or coroutine. It requires four parameters: the procedure name of the process, the base address and size of the workspace for the process, and a variable of type PROCESS to which the new process is assigned.

The procedure must be declared at the global (outermost) level without parameters. The workspace contains the coroutine's local variables, procedure-call information, and suspended execution state. The size of this space is determined by adding the procedure's data size to the data sizes of any called procedures, plus allowances for procedure-call linkages. In general, it is best to allocate generous storage space to coroutines.

Coroutine calls are invoked through the TRANSFER procedure. Its syntax is

```
PROCEDURE TRANSFER (VAR p1,
                         p2 : PROCESS);
```

TRANSFER suspends the current process, establishes the process identified by the variable p2 as the next process, saves the execution state of the current process in the PROCESS variable p1, and then resumes execution with the new process. If the p2 process is being invoked for the first time, execution begins with the first statement in the procedure body. Otherwise, execution is resumed after the TRANSFER statement that previously gave up control.

p2 must have been assigned a process through NEWPROCESS or the TRANSFER will produce unpredictable results.

TRANSFER can also be used to terminate a coroutine by returning control to the main calling module. Another, more abrupt, method of termination occurs if control reaches the end of a coroutine procedure. In this case, the entire program is terminated.

Coroutines often find application in handling device interrupts. They are invoked to service the interrupt, then suspended until another interrupt occurs. Because the occurrence of a device interrupt falls outside of the program's control, there must be a way of invoking the coroutine other than explicit transfer from within the program. The procedure

IOTRANSFER from the SYSTEM module is designed to handle this situation.

IOTRANSFER closely resembles TRANSFER. It suspends the current process and activates the new process. The next interrupt, however, causes an unscheduled transfer back to the original process.

Because computer systems are usually comprised of several devices with different levels of interrupts, Modula-2 supports *module priorities*. A system-dependent module priority is specified by following the module name with a CARDINAL value in brackets indicating the priority. For example,

MODULE Printer[4];

specifies a priority of 4. The greater the number, the higher the priority.

A program can be interrupted if and only if the interrupting device has a priority greater than the priority level of the module executing currently. In other words, an interrupt from a hardware device with a priority of 9 will suspend execution of a module with priority level 3. The module specified for priority 9 will then be executed.

The priority of each device is defined in hardware and the priority of each module is specified in the module heading. Modules lacking a priority specification have null priority. When called, they inherit the calling module's priority.

IOTRANSFER and module priorities are illustrated in Program 6–5, which serves as a device driver for a printer. This program sends characters to a printer device through a 20-character buffer. After the printer prints a character, it generates an interrupt to indicate that it is ready for another.

Program 6–5 Printer

```
DEFINITION MODULE Printer;
    EXPORT QUALIFIED Print;          (* Print is called from external *)
    PROCEDURE Print(ch : CHAR);      (* module *)
END Printer.
```

```
IMPLEMENTATION MODULE Printer[4]; (* Set module priority = 4 *)

FROM SYSTEM IMPORT WORD,
                   PROCESS,
                   ADR,
                   SIZE,
                   NEWPROCESS,
                   TRANSFER,
                   IOTRANSFER,
                   LISTEN;
```

```
CONST
  BufSize = 2Ø;              (* buffer size *)

VAR
  BufNum : INTEGER;          (* number of characters in buffer *)
  buffer : ARRAY [1..BufSize] OF CHAR;
  inslot,                    (* buffer slot for input *)
  outslot : [1..BufSize];    (* buffer slot for output *)
  pro,                       (* producer *)
  con : PROCESS;             (* consumer, printer driver *)
  wsp : ARRAY [1..1ØØ] OF WORD;    (* process workspace *)
  PrtrStat[ØFF74H] : BITSET;       (* printer status *)
  PrtrData[ØFF76H] : CHAR;         (* printer data *)

PROCEDURE Print(ch : CHAR);        (* put char in buffer, wait if
                                      full *)
BEGIN
  INC(BufNum);                     (* increment chars in buffer *)
  WHILE (BufNum > BufSize) DO      (* buffer full? *)
    LISTEN;     (* yes—wait for driver to remove a char *)
  END;     (* WHILE *)
  buffer[inslot] := ch;            (* put char in buffer *)
  inslot := (inslot MOD BufSize) + 1;     (* increment input slot *)
  IF (BufNum = Ø) THEN             (* was buffer empty before this
                                      char? *)
    TRANSFER(pro,con);             (* yes—start driver *)
  END;     (* IF *)
END Print;

PROCEDURE PrintDriver;             (* print char(s) in buffer *)
BEGIN
  LOOP
    DEC(BufNum);                   (* decrement chars in buffer *)
    IF (BufNum < Ø) THEN           (* buffer empty? *)
      TRANSFER(con,pro);           (* yes—exit driver *)
    END;     (* IF *)
    PrtrData := buffer[outslot];   (* move char from buffer to
                                      printer *)
    outslot := (outslot MOD BufSize) + 1;     (* increment out slot *)
    PrtrStat := {6};               (* enable device interrupt *)
    IOTRANSFER(con,pro,34H);       (* return to next instruction upon *)
```

```
        PrtrStat := { };              (* output completion & disable *)
    END;      (* LOOP *)             (* interrupts *)
  END PrintDriver;

  BEGIN       (* main module *)
    BufNum := 0;
    inslot := 1;
    outslot := 1;
    NEWPROCESS(PrintDriver,ADR(wsp),SIZE(wsp),con);
    TRANSFER(pro,con);     (* invoke driver & set transfer address *)
  END Printer.                (* for subsequent calls from Print *)
```

Procedure Print puts a character in the buffer and invokes the coroutine, PrintDriver. If the buffer is full, Print sits in a WHILE loop executing
the procedure LISTEN, which is imported from module SYSTEM. LISTEN
allows IOTRANSFERs to occur.

Procedure Print is invoked by an external call. Observe that it appears
in the definition module export list.

The fixed-address variables PtrStat and PtrData access the memory
mapped status and data registers of the printer.

The IOTRANSFER in the procedure PrintDriver suspends the procedure
after a character is sent to the printer. The call to IOTRANSFER includes
the vector address assigned to the printer device. These addresses are, of
course, system-dependent.

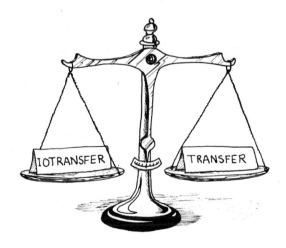

6.5 Summary/Problems

The types and procedures of module SYSTEM provide machine-level operations, including concurrent processing, type conversion, address arithmetic, bit manipulation, and direct access to memory. They allow high-level programs to control the machine at a low level. Because the low-level facilities circumvent the normal strict enforcement of types, the programmer must assume responsibility for data integrity.

Although the machine-specific nature of SYSTEM is a benefit for intricate interfacing with underlying hardware, it detracts from a program's portability. Programs that rely heavily on the architecture of the hardware tie themselves to a single kind of machine.

SYSTEM, like other modules, is accessed through an IMPORT statement, but it is actually integral to the compiler. To distinguish it from the external library modules, it is called a *pseudomodule*.

The balance of this chapter covered the advantages of delegating program logic to *local* and *separately compiled modules*. Separately compiled modules consist of DEFINITION and IMPLEMENTATION parts. The definition part hosts the module's interface or export list. The implementation part hides operational details, including the components of *opaque types*.

With the exception of a few variations of the core grammar and vocabulary, this book has now covered Modula-2 from head to toe. What details remain are included in Appendix A, the language reference, which systematically describes the entire language.

The next chapter presents a quick primer for skippers who are already fluent in the operation of Modula-2's predecessor, Pascal.

Problems

1. [M] Through research and/or experimentation, find the size in bits of variables of the following types on your computer system:

    INTEGER   POINTER
    CARDINAL   PROCEDURE
    BOOLEAN   Opaque
    CHAR   WORD
    REAL   ADDRESS
    BITSET   PROCESS

2. [M]Consider the following definition and implementation modules:

    DEFINITION MODULE Numbers;
    EXPORT QUALIFIED amount;
    TYPE
       amount;
    END Numbers.

```
IMPLEMENTATION MODULE Numbers;
TYPE
    amount : CARDINAL;
    . . .
END Numbers.
```

Will the multiplication statement in the following importing module work? Why or why not?

```
MODULE ProcessNumbers;
FROM Numbers IMPORT amount;
VAR
    qty : amount;
BEGIN
    qty := qty * 3;
END ProcessNumbers.
```

3. [M] Modify the coroutine demonstration in Program 6–4 to terminate by returning to the main module after the second procedure displays its message 25 times.

4. [S] Some 200 years ago Wolfgang von Kempelen, a Hungarian inventor, toured Europe with a machine called the Maezel Chess Automaton. The chess-playing machine took on all comers and defeated most of them. Among its admirers was Edgar Allan Poe, who speculated in an essay on how the device worked. A few years later, the "mechanism" was revealed. Hidden within the machine was a legless Polish army officer named Worouski, a master chess player.

   Today, enterprising inventors are still trying to develop a mechanical chess player. A cash sum of $100,000 has been offered for the first person to design a computer program that wins the World Chess Championship. Write a chess-playing program. If it clinches the world title, contact Professor Edward Fredkin at the Massachusetts Institute of Technology for your reward.

7.

Quick
Primer
for
Pascal
Skippers

7. Quick Primer for Pascal Skippers

*M*ore than one programmer has asked why Niklaus Wirth didn't name Pascal's successor Pascal-2 instead of Modula-2. After all, the languages look so alike that in many cases you need a magnifying glass to distinguish an algorithm coded in Modula-2 from the same one coded in Pascal. A comparison of Modula-2 and Pascal implementations of the Sieve of Eratosthenes algorithm remarkably highlights the similarities between the languages (see Program 7–1). Without the subtle differences that are underlined in Program 7–1, a casual comparison might lead you to conclude that the two implementations were identical.

Program 7–1 Prime

```
MODULE Prime;   (* Modula-2 *)       PROGRAM Prime;   (* Pascal *)
FROM InOut IMPORT
  WriteLn,
  WriteInt,
  WriteString;
CONST                                CONST
  Flg Size = 8190;                     Flg Size = 8190
VAR                                  VAR
  Flags : ARRAY[0..Flg Size] OF        Flags : ARRAY[0..Flg Size] of
       BOOLEAN;                             BOOLEAN;
  I,                                   I,
  K,                                   K,
  Prime,                               Prime,
  Count,                               Count,
  Iter : INTEGER;                      Iter : INTEGER;
BEGIN                                BEGIN
  WriteLn;
  WriteString('10 iterations');        writeln('10 iterations');
  FOR Iter := 1 TO 10 DO               FOR Iter := 1 TO 10 DO
```

```
Count := 0;                          BEGIN
FOR I := 0 TO Flg Size DO             Count := 0;
                                      FOR I := 0 TO Flg Size DO
   Flags[I] := TRUE                    BEGIN
   END;                                 Flags[I] := TRUE
FOR I := 0 TO Flg Size DO              END;
                                      FOR I := 0 TO Flg Size DO
   IF Flags[I] THEN                     BEGIN
                                        IF Flags[I] THEN
   Prime := I+I+3;                       BEGIN
   K := I+Prime;                         Prime := I+I+3;
   WHILE K <= Flg Size DO                K : I+Prime;
                                         WHILE K <= Flg Size DO
      Flags[K] := FALSE;                  BEGIN
      K := K + Prime                       Flags[K] := FALSE;
      END;   (* WHILE *)                    K := K + Prime
      Count := Count + 1                    END;   (* WHILE *)
      END;   (* IF *)                       Count := Count + 1
      END;   (* FOR I *)                     END;   (* IF *)
   END;   (* FOR Iter *)                     END;   (* FOR I *)
WriteLn;                                  END;   (* FOR Iter *)
WriteInt(Count,6);
WriteString(' primes');
END Prime.                             writeln(Count,' primes')
                                      END.   (* Prime *)
```

Despite the resemblance between the two languages, there are syntactical variations and conceptual enhancements that clearly set Modula-2 apart from its older sibling. This chapter presents a quick primer for the programmer schooled in Pascal who would like to approach Modula-2 from the familiar and not-too-distant territory of its predecessor. The primer focuses on the major distinctions, leaving comprehensive discussion of the nuts and bolts of Modula-2 to the other chapters.

The first inconsistency confronts the Pascal skipper at line one of every program. Modula-2 programs start with the reserved word MODULE instead of PROGRAM. The module name must also accompany the END statement, as shown in the program for the Sieve algorithm.

Following the MODULE statement, constants, types, variables, and procedures may be mixed in any order, which is different from Pascal's strict sequence of CONST, TYPE, VAR, and so on. This flexibility allows related declarations to be grouped together.

Modula-2 relaxes Pascal's restrictions on constants. Constant expressions may be used wherever constants are expected. The statement

DisplayScreen : ARRAY[1..(24*80)] OF CHAR;

defines an array with 1920 character elements. Numeric constants may be specified as octal or hexadecimal in addition to decimal by appending the letter *B* or *H*—for example, 0377B and 0FFH.

The preceding array declaration also illustrates Modula-2's sensitivity to upper- and lower-case characters. Reserved words *must* be capitalized. Identifiers are case-sensitive, too. For example, COUNT is considered distinct from Count and count. By convention, programmer-defined identifiers are comprised of all lower-case or mixed upper- and lower-case characters to distinguish such identifiers from reserved words. To prevent accidental assignments of aliases, *all* characters of identifiers, instead of just the first eight, are regarded as significant.

The final point distinguishing Modula-2 identifiers from those used in Pascal involves special characters. Modula-2's identifiers are composed of only letters and digits. The common Pascal practice of embedding special characters, such as underscores, within identifiers, is *illegal* in Modula-2.

Modula-2 augments the standard types INTEGER, REAL, CHAR, and BOOLEAN with the unsigned integer type CARDINAL. CARDINAL is the preferred type for non-negative integer operations.

For displaying variables of these types, Pascal conveniently offers the generic output procedure writeln. Strictly speaking, Modula-2 contains no input or output. Instead, I/O is delegated to standard library modules to avoid system dependencies. What is written in Pascal as

writeln('Category = ',categ,' Quantity = ',qty:3);

becomes in Modula-2

```
WriteString("Category = ");
WriteInt(categ,0);
WriteString(" Quantity = ");
WriteInt(qty,3);
WriteLn;      (* write carriage return/line feed *)
```

The procedures WriteString, WriteInt, and WriteLn are *imported* from the *module library*. Library modules are compiled separately and are bound to a program at execution time. The type interfaces between program and module variables are checked for integrity at both compilation and execution. Overall, the concept of modules is the single most important feature distinguishing Modula-2 from Pascal.

The I/O example just given points out two other changes. Modula-2's strings may be indicated by either double or single quotation marks. The latter permit double quotation marks to be embedded in strings.

The curly brace symbols, { and }, no longer delimit comments; they now represent set delimiters. Besides the delimiter symbol, Modula-2's sets deviate from Pascal's in two other areas. Sets are generally small—the size of one machine word—and the elements must be constant expressions. The second restriction is somewhat mitigated by the standard procedures INCL and EXCL, which include and exclude elements from sets. The elements in INCL and EXCL statements may be constants *or variables.*

The compound symbols (* and *) replace curly braces as comment delimiters. Unlike Pascal, Modula-2, comments can be nested. An example of a nested comment follows:

```
WriteString("Category = ");      (* (* display category *) *)
```

Nested comments allow parts of a program already containing comments to be commented out easily. They also prevent improperly matched comment delimiters from subtly converting instructions to comments, as would happen if the following statements were executed in Pascal:

```
MODULE DoSqrt;
  . . .
  ReadReal(x);     (* get number *   )
  y := sqrt(x);    (* find square root *)
  WriteReal(sqrt(x),10);
  . . .
END DoSqrt.
```

Pascal accepts this sequence, but the assignment statement is regarded as a comment because a space occurs within the first ending comment delimiter following the word "number." Modula-2, on the other hand, would detect the mismatched comment delimiters and indicate an error.

Other syntactical improvements include explicit termination symbols for IF, FOR, WHILE, and REPEAT. The first three are terminated by END. REPEAT finishes with a corresponding UNTIL statement. The BEGIN/END construct is eliminated, meaning there is less worrying about tidying up semicolons.

In addition to the repetitive instructions FOR, WHILE, and REPEAT, Modula-2 offers LOOP. LOOP best expresses infinite repetition and, when combined with the EXIT statement, allows the loop to be terminated at places other than the beginning or end. EXIT handles situations previously addressed by Pascal's GOTO statement, which Modula-2 dropped.

The FOR and CASE statements have been strengthened through additional clauses. Step values other than 1 may be specified for use in the

FOR statement with the optional BY part:

```
FOR i := 80 TO 20 BY -2 DO
    . . .
```

Negative step values take care of the same functions as performed by Pascal's DOWNTO clause, which has been eliminated.

The ELSE part of the CASE statement catches unspecified values. For example,

```
CASE ch OF
    "0".."9" : HavNumber; |
    "A".."Z",
    "a".."z" : HavLetter;
ELSE
    HavOther;
END;
```

This example also illustrates Modula-2's acceptance of subranges as case values and the | symbol, which means "or" in the CASE statement.

Boolean expressions in Modula-2 generally resemble those of Pascal, except that the evaluation of compound expressions will be terminated if the result can be determined from the first argument. Short circuiting the evaluation in this manner produces valid results even if the second operand is undefined. For instance,

```
IF ((NumPeople # 0) AND (TotalWeight/NumPeople > 150))
    THEN
        . . .
```

The remaining Modula-2 constructs not found in Pascal constitute major design enhancements. Concurrent and interrupt processes may be programmed through *coroutines*. Coroutines depend on system-dependent procedures imported from module SYSTEM.

SYSTEM also hosts types and procedures related to the computer's hardware architecture. These facilities permit applications that had previously fallen in the domain of assembly language to be written in the high-level elegance of Modula-2.

Appendices

A. Language Reference

A.1 Symbols

Identifiers are composed of letters and digits. The first character must be a letter. Modula-2 imposes no limit on the length of identifiers.

Numeric values are written as either whole or real numbers. Whole numbers are interpreted as decimal, octal, hexadecimal, or character-equivalent, depending on the suffix:

Modula-2 whole number	decimal equivalent	
248	248	no suffix indicates decimal
370B	248	B indicates octal
0F8H	248	H indicates hexadecimal

If a hexadecimal number begins with *A* through *F*, it must be preceded by a 0 to distinguish it from an identifier.

The letter *C* appended to an integer indicates the character that is identified in ASCII code by the given octal ordinal number. For example, 15C denotes a carriage return and 101C denotes the letter "A." The *C* suffix is useful for representing nondisplayable characters such as carriage return and line feed.

Real numbers always contain a decimal point. They may also be expressed exponentially. Exponential notation takes the form

$\pm$x.xxxxxxEspp

where $\pm$x.xxxxxx is a decimal number between $\pm$1.0000000 and $\pm$9.9999999, *s* is the sign of the power (absent or plus for positive, minus for negative), and *pp* is the exponent or power of 10. For example, the decimal value nine can be expressed as 9.0 or 0.9E01.

Strings are sequences of characters enclosed in double or single quotation marks. A string must not extend beyond the end of a line. Valid strings are

"Enter AMOUNT: "
"Enter AMOUNT in format 'xxx.xx': "

Character strings of length 1 are of type CHAR. Strings greater than one character are regarded as arrays—in particular, a string of length *n* is treated as

ARRAY[Ø..n-1] OF CHAR;

Operators and *delimiters* are special characters, character pairs, and reserved words (see Table A–1). Operators and delimiters consisting of more than one character must be written without intervening spaces.

Table A–1 Modula-2 Operators and Delimiters

Operator/ Delimiter	Description
+	addition
	set union
−	subtraction
	set difference
*	multiplication
	set intersection
/	real division
	symmetric set difference
DIV	integer division
MOD	modulus, remainder of integer division
IN	set membership

Operator/ Delimiter	*Description*
:=	assignment in executable instruction
=	equal (boolean comparison)
	assignment in constant declaration
	assignment in type declaration
<	less than (boolean comparison)
>	greater than (boolean comparison)
#	not equal (boolean comparison)
<>	not equal (boolean comparison)
<=	less than or equal to (boolean comparison)
	contained in (subset)
>=	greater than or equal to (boolean comparison)
	contains (superset)
&	boolean and (conjunction)
AND	boolean and (conjunction)
OR	boolean or (disjunction)
~	boolean negation
NOT	boolean negation
;	separate statements
:	separate variable name and type
	separate case labels and case statements
.	decimal point
	module terminator
	record field selector
	qualified identifier selector
,	separate identifiers
	separate array indexes
↑	pointer dereferencing
|	delimiter for CASE and RECORD variants
(	start nested expression
	start parameter list
	start enumeration
)	end nested expression
	end parameter list
	end enumeration
[	start index list
	start subrange
	start variable absolute address
	start module priority

Operator/ Delimiter	Description
]	end index list
	end subrange
	end variable absolute address
	end module priority
{	start set expression
}	end set expression
(*	start comment
*)	end comment
..	subrange specifier

Parentheses should be used to clearly indicate the precedence of operators where multiple operators appear. In expressions without parentheses, operator precedence is relative to four classes of operators:

first (highest)	NOT ~
second	* / DIV MOD AND &
third	+ − OR
fourth (lowest)	= # <> < <= > >= IN

If sequences of operators of the same precedence class occur, the evaluation is made from left to right.

The following 40 *reserved words* must not be used as identifiers:

AND	FOR	QUALIFIED
ARRAY	FROM	RECORD
BEGIN	IF	REPEAT
BY	IMPLEMENTATION	RETURN
CASE	IMPORT	SET
CONST	IN	THEN
DEFINITION	LOOP	TO
DIV	MOD	TYPE
DO	MODULE	UNTIL
ELSE	NOT	VAR
ELSIF	OF	WHILE
END	OR	WITH
EXIT	POINTER	
EXPORT	PROCEDURE	

A.2 Constant Declarations

The reserved word CONST denotes a constant declaration. Constants may consist of numbers, expressions, characters, or strings. An example of the use of constants follows:

```
CONST
  ScreenWidth = 80;
  ScreenSize = ScreenWidth * 24;
  msg = "Aye, Aye!";
  ingredients = {cocoa,coconut,sugar};
```

A.3 Type Declarations

The reserved word TYPE denotes a type declaration. In general, a type declaration of the form

```
TYPE
  abc = SomeType;
VAR
  SomeVar : abc;
```

can be abbreviated to

```
VAR
  SomeVar : SomeType;
```

but the former construction aids program maintenance.

Figure A–1 illustrates the possible types and their classifications.

Unstructured types are labeled as such because they are atomic; that is, they consist of no component types. *Standard types* represent predesignated values. Descriptions of the unstructured, standard types follow with sample type declarations:

INTEGER   positive and negative whole numbers.
```
  i = INTEGER;
```

LONGINT   positive and negative whole numbers of greater range than INTEGER.
```
  bigi = LONGINT;
```

CARDINAL   non-negative whole numbers.
```
  c = CARDINAL;
```

LONGCARD   non-negative whole numbers of greater range than CARDINAL.
```
  bigc = LONGCARD;
```

Figure A–1 Possible Types and Their
Classifications

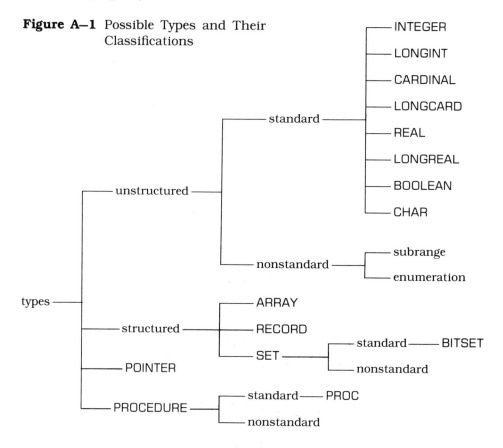

REAL   numbers with fractional parts.
                r = REAL;

LONGREAL   numbers with fractional parts of greater range
                than REAL.
                bigr = LONGREAL;

BOOLEAN   truth values indicated by the standard identifiers
                TRUE and FALSE.
                EndOfFile = BOOLEAN;

CHAR   one of the 128 ASCII characters.
                initial = CHAR;

Nonstandard types are programmer-defined. The unstructured, nonstandard types include

enumeration list of identifiers associated with a variable. Each identifier corresponds to a cardinal value.

weekdays = (Mon, Tue, Wed, Thu, Fri);

subrange segment of unstructured, standard types, except that REAL and LONGREAL subranges are prohibited. The value of the lower limit determines the base type as follows:

non-negative number = CARDINAL
negative number = INTEGER
character = CHAR

month = [1..31];
temp = [−12..61];
capletters = ["A".."Z"];

The standard functions MIN and MAX return the minimum and maximum values of any unstructured type including REAL and LONGREAL. On most 16-bit computers, INTEGER ranges from −32,768 to 32,767, CARDINAL ranges from 0 to 65,535, and REAL ranges from −1.7014E38 to +1.7014E38.

Structured types are comprised, or *structured*, of elements of the unstructured types. They include

ARRAY fixed-size group of elements of same *component* type accessed through an *index*. Index must be subrange or enumeration.

StateName = ARRAY[1..25] OF CHAR;
AllStateNames = ARRAY[1..50] OF
ARRAY[1..25] OF CHAR;

RECORD group of elements of different component types and possibly varying sizes (RECORD variant).

date =
RECORD
month : ARRAY[1..9] OF CHAR;
day : [1..31];
year : CARDINAL;
END;

address =
RECORD

```
dept : ARRAY[1..10] OF CHAR;
CASE DoorAddr : BOOLEAN OF
   TRUE : StreetNo : CARDINAL;
            StreetName : ARRAY[1..25] OF
                                    CHAR; |
      FALSE : BoxNo : CARDINAL;
   END;
END;
```

SET   group of values of a subrange or enumeration. Most implementations limit the size of a set to the word size of the host computer. The standard type BITSET designates SET OF [0..w−1] where w is the word size.

```
boatparts = (hull,mast,deck,rudder);
boat = SET OF boatparts;
DeviceStatus = BITSET;
```

The final two types form their own categories, fitting into neither unstructured nor structured types:

POINTER   link to a variable of any given type. The standard identifier NIL designates a value pointing to nothing.

```
AgePntr = POINTER TO AgeNode;
AgeNode =
   RECORD
      CrewMemAge : CARDINAL;
      NextAge : AgePntr;
   END;
```

PROCEDURE used to declare a procedure variable. The standard type PROC designates a procedure that has no parameters.

```
Display = PROCEDURE(CARDINAL,
                              CARDINAL);
DoLineFeed = PROC;
```

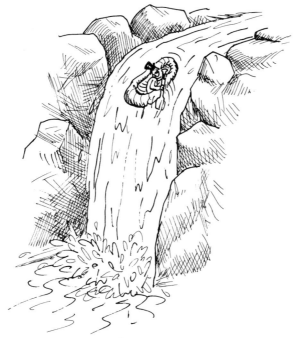

A.4 Variable Declarations

Variable declarations introduce data identifers and their types. Multiple variables of the same type can be declared by listing their identifiers, separated by commas. For example,

```
i,
j,
k : INTEGER;
count : CARDINAL;
```

A.5 Statements

A statement performs an activity. *Statement sequences* are one or more statements separated by semicolons. Modula-2's statements and their descriptions follow.

Assignment

The assignment operator, :=, means "takes on" or "becomes." The variable on the left side of the assignment takes on the value on the right side.

The operand types must be *assignment-compatible.* Operands are assignment-compatible if their types are identical or if both are subranges of the same type. Types INTEGER and CARDINAL (and their subranges) are also assignment-compatible, although they are not compatible in expressions.

If a string is assigned to a longer string variable, null characters, CHR(0), are padded on the destination. A string is defined as a zero-based character array. An example follows:

```
VAR
   port : ARRAY[0..6] OF CHAR;
 . . .
   port := "NY";      (* pads five nulls after "NY" *)
```

Procedure Call

A procedure call consists of a procedure identifier or procedure-variable identifier, possibly followed by a list of parameters. Lack of parentheses or empty parentheses indicate a procedure that has no parameters. For example,

```
WriteLn;
```

is equivalent to

```
WriteLn( );
```

A *function procedure* call without parameters *must* include empty parentheses.

```
IF
```

The general form is

```
IF condition-1 THEN statement-sequence-1
ELSIF condition-2 THEN statement-sequence-2
 . . .
ELSIF condition-n-1 THEN statement-sequence-n-1
ELSE statement-sequence
END;
```

Condition-1 through condition-n-1 are boolean expressions that are evaluated sequentially. When the first true condition is reached, the corresponding statement sequence is executed and the remainder of the IF statement, if any, is ignored. If none of the conditions is satisfied, the statement sequence following the ELSE clause is executed. The ELSIF and ELSE clauses are optional.

The following examples show how the IF statement can be used:

```
IF (temp <= 98.6) THEN
   WriteString("temperature ok");
END;

IF (temp <= 98.6) THEN
   WriteString("temperature ok");
ELSIF (temp < 101.0) THEN
   WriteString("mild fever");
END;

IF (temp <= 98.6) THEN
   WriteString("temperature ok");
ELSIF (temp < 101.0) THEN
   WriteString("mild fever");
ELSE
   WriteString("moderate to severe fever");
END;
```

CASE

The general form is

```
CASE expression OF
   case-1 : statement-sequence-1; |
   case-2 : statement-sequence-2; |
   . . .
   case-n : statement-sequence-n;
ELSE
   statement-sequence;
END;
```

Case labels case-1 through case-n are constants or constant expressions that are evaluated sequentially. When the first case label matching the value of the case expression is reached, the corresponding statement sequence is executed and the remainder of the CASE statement, if any, is ignored. The optional ELSE clause covers the situation in which none of the case labels matches the expression. If the CASE contains no ELSE clause and none of the case labels matches, an error message will be generated during execution of the program.

The case expression can be any unstructured type except for REAL and LONGREAL. The case labels must be compatible with that type.

The following example illustrates the use of the CASE statement:

```
CASE ch OF
  "0".."9": WriteString ("digit"); |
  "A".."Z": WriteString ("upper-case character");
ELSE
  WriteString("miscellaneous character");
END;
```

WHILE

The general form is

```
WHILE boolean expression DO
  statement sequence
END;
```

The expression, which must be Boolean, is evaluated before each execution of the statement sequence. If it is true, the statement sequence is executed. Otherwise, the WHILE loop is terminated. WHILE loops allow the possibility that the statement sequence may not be executed at all if the value of the Boolean expression is false at the first execution cycle.

The following is an example of the use of WHILE:

```
WHILE (i >= 0) DO
  a[i] := a[i] + 5;
  DEC(i);
END;
```

REPEAT

The general form is

```
REPEAT
  statement sequence
UNTIL boolean expression;
```

The boolean expression is evaluated after each execution of the statement sequence. If it is true, the REPEAT loop is terminated. Otherwise, the statement sequence is repeated. REPEAT loops execute at least once. An example follows:

```
REPEAT
  a[i] := a[i] + 5;
  DEC(i);
UNTIL (i < 0);
```

FOR

The general form is

```
FOR control-variable := expression-1 TO expression-2 BY
                        constant-expression DO
    statement sequence
END;
```

The statement sequence is executed while the control variable ranges from expression-1 to expression-2. The control variable is incremented or decremented by the value of the constant-expression. A positive value causes an increment; a negative value causes a decrement. If the constant-expression is not specified, an increment of 1 is assumed.

If the constant-expression is an increment, the FOR loop terminates when the control variable increases to greater than expression-2. In this case, if expression-1 is greater than expression-2, the loop will not be executed at all.

If the constant-expression is a decrement, the loop terminates when the control variable decreases to less than expression-2. In this case, if expression-1 is less than expression-2, the loop will not be executed at all.

The types of expression-1 and expression-2 can be any unstructured types with the exception of REAL and LONGREAL, and they must be compatible with the control variable. The control variable cannot be a parameter declared in a procedure heading, part of a structured variable, or imported.

The constant-expression must be a constant of type INTEGER or CARDINAL. Some examples follow:

```
FOR i := 10 TO 0 BY −1 DO
  a[i] := a[i] + 5;
END;

FOR ch := "a" to "z" BY 1 DO
  Write(ch);
END;
```

LOOP

The general form is

```
LOOP
   statement sequence
END;
```

The statement sequence is repeated until an EXIT instruction is executed within the sequence. If no EXIT is executed, the loop will be repeated continuously. LOOP most often expresses operations that must be terminated in the middle of the statement sequence or activity that is terminated externally. An example follows:

```
LOOP       (* calculate roots until negative value is encountered *)
   ReadReal(x);           (* get value *)
   IF (x < 0.0) THEN      (* non-negative ? *)
     EXIT;                (* yes—quit *)
   END;
   WriteReal(sqrt(x),10);  (* calculate square root and display it *)
END;                      (* do another *)
```

RETURN

RETURN serves two purposes. In procedures and modules, it terminates the enclosing body. In function procedures, it also relays a result to the calling statement. The result type must be assignment-compatible with the function type.

An example of terminating a procedure follows:

```
PROCEDURE DoSqrt;
  . . .
   LOOP       (* calculate roots until negative value is encountered *)
      ReadReal(x);           (* get value *)
      IF (x < 0.0) THEN      (* nonnegative? *)
        RETURN;              (* yes—return *)
      END;
      WriteReal(sqrt(x),10);  (* calculate square root and display *)
   END;       (* LOOP *)      (* do another *)
END DoSqrt;
```

The following is an example of terminating a procedure and returning a function result:

```
PROCEDURE Factorial(k : CARDINAL) : CARDINAL;
  VAR
    i,
    f : CARDINAL;
  BEGIN
    f := 1;
    FOR i := 1 TO k BY 1 DO
      f := f * i;
    END;
    RETURN f;
  END Factorial;
```

WITH

The general form is

```
WITH record variable DO
  statement sequence
END;
```

The RECORD variable name is automatically prefixed to field identifiers of the record within the statement sequence. For example, given the declaration

```
TYPE
  sailboat =
    RECORD
      masts : [1..5];
      yearsold : CARDINAL;
      skippername : ARRAY[1..25] OF CHAR;
    END;
  VAR
    schooner : sailboat;
```

the statements

```
WITH schooner DO
  masts := 3;
  yearsold := 15;
  skippername := "Black Beard";
END;
```

are equivalent to

```
schooner.masts := 3;
schooner.yearsold := 15;
schooner.skippername := "Black Beard";
```

A.6 Procedure Declarations

A procedure declaration consists of a *procedure heading* and a *procedure body*. The heading includes the procedure identifier and *formal parameters*. The body encompasses the *local* declarations and statements.

The formal parameters serve as place holders for the *actual* parameters that are passed by the calling statement. Procedure parameters fall into two classes, *variable* and *value* parameters. Using variable parameters, the procedure can modify the contents of the actual parameters in the calling statement. Variable parameters are indicated by the prefix VAR in the procedure heading.

Value parameters receive copies of the actual parameters. They do not affect the contents of the actual parameters. Value parameters are indicated by the absence of a VAR prefix in the procedure heading. An example follows:

```
PROCEDURE ConDay(VAR JulDay : CARDINAL;    (* variable parm *)
                     day : CARDINAL;        (* value parm *)
                     mm : ARRAY[1..9]
                     OF CHAR);              (* value parm *)
```

The types of the actual and formal parameters must agree. Specifically, the types of variable parameters must be identical; value parameter types need only be assignment-compatible.

A formal parameter may be an *open array* parameter, which is an array with no explicit upper index. The general form of an open array is

```
name : ARRAY OF T;
```

where name is the array identifier and T is an arbitrary base type.

Open arrays are zero-based. If an actual parameter array of the form

```
a : ARRAY[m..n] OF CHAR;
```

is passed to an open array parameter, the index of the open array would be [0..(n-m)].

Open arrays must be accessed element by element; they cannot be accessed as units except to be placed in procedure parameter lists. Another restriction involves the number of dimensions—for practical purposes, open array parameters may have only one dimension.

An example of an open-array parameter follows:

```
CONST
  greeting = "Ahoy there";
  . . .
```

```
PROCEDURE WriteString(s : ARRAY OF CHAR);
 . . .
WriteString(greeting);
```

Overall, procedures belong to one of two categories: *proper procedures* or *function procedures. Function procedures* have an unstructured result type and relay the result to the calling statement through a RETURN statement. *Proper procedures* do not have result types.

An example of a function procedure follows:

```
PROCEDURE Power(t : REAL;
                e : CARDINAL) : REAL;
VAR
   xy : REAL;
 . . .
   RETURN xy;
END Power;
```

A.7 Standard Functions and Procedures

Standard functions and procedures are integral to the language and need not be imported. Tables A–2 and A–3 summarize their operations.

Table A–2   Standard Functions

name	argument type	result type	description
ABS(x)	INTEGER LONGINT REAL LONGREAL	Same as argument	Returns absolute value
CAP(ch)	CHAR	CHAR	Returns upper-case equivalent of lower-case character; upper-case and nonalphabetic characters are returned unchanged

name	argument type	result type	description
CHR(x)	CARDINAL LONGCARD	CHAR	Returns character equivalent of CARDINAL value: CHR(x) = VAL(CHAR,x)
FLOAT(x)	CARDINAL LONGCARD	REAL	Converts CARDINAL x to REAL value
HIGH(a)	ARRAY	CARDINAL	Returns upper bound of first dimension of array
MAX(T)	CARDINAL LONGCARD INTEGER LONGINT REAL LONGREAL CHAR enumeration	Same as argument	Returns maximum value of type T
MIN(T)	CARDINAL LONGCARD INTEGER LONGINT REAL LONGREAL CHAR enumeration	Same as argument	Returns minimum value of type T
ODD(x)	CARDINAL LONGCARD INTEGER LONGINT	BOOLEAN	Returns TRUE if x is odd; returns FALSE if not

name	argument type	result type	description
ORD(x)	CARDINAL LONGCARD INTEGER LONGINT CHAR enumeration	CARDINAL	Returns ordinal value of x (0 origin)
TRUNC(x)	REAL LONGREAL	CARDINAL	Truncates x to its integral part
VAL(T,x)	T = CARDINAL LONGCARD INTEGER LONGINT CHAR enumeration x = CARDINAL	Same as T	Returns value with ordinal number x (0 origin) and type T VAL(T,ORD(x)) = x

Table A–3 Standard Procedures

name	argument type	description
DEC(x)	CARDINAL LONGCARD INTEGER LONGINT CHAR enumeration	x := x − 1
DEC(x,n)	CARDINAL LONGCARD INTEGER LONGINT CHAR enumeration	x := x − n
DISPOSE(p)	POINTER	Deallocates storage allotted to p where p is declared as POINTER TO T. DISPOSE is automatically translated into DEALLOCATE(p,TSIZE(T)). The standard library module Storage normally provides DEALLOCATE, but it may also be programmed explicitly.
DISPOSE (p,t1,t2,...)	p = POINTER t1, t2, ... = tag fields	Deallocates storage allotted to tag fields t1, t2, ... in T where p is declared as POINTER TO T. DISPOSE is automatically translated into DEALLOCATE (p,TSIZE(T,t1,t2,...)). The standard library module Storage normally provides DEALLOCATE, but it may also be programmed explicitly.

name	argument type	description
EXCL(s,i)	SET	Excludes element i from SET s. Element i is a constant or variable expression of the base type of s. s := s − {i}
HALT		Terminates program
INC(x)	CARDINAL LONGCARD INTEGER LONGINT CHAR enumeration	x := x + 1
INC(x,n)	CARDINAL LONGCARD INTEGER LONGINT CHAR enumeration	x := x + n

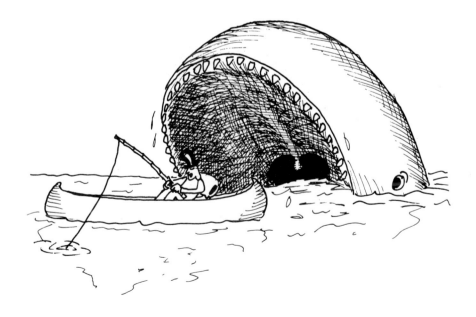

name	argument type	description
INCL(s,i)	SET	Includes element i into SET s. Element i is a constant or variable expression of the base type of s. s := s + {i}
NEW(p)	POINTER	Obtains storage for p where p is declared as POINTER TO T. NEW is automatically translated into ALLOCATE(p,TSIZE(T)). The standard library module Storage normally provides ALLOCATE, but it may also be programmed explicitly.
NEW (p,t1,t2,...)	p = POINTER t1, t2, ... = tag fields	Obtains storage for tag fields t1, t2, ... in T where p is declared as POINTER TO T. NEW is automatically translated into ALLOCATE (p,TSIZE(T,t1,t2,...)). The standard library module Storage normally provides ALLOCATE, but it may also be programmed explicitly.

A.8 Modules

A module is a collection of declarations and a sequence of statements enclosed by the reserved words MODULE and END. If the module identifier in the MODULE statement is followed by a CARDINAL value in the form

    MODULE Printer[4];

then that value is taken as the module's priority for use in conjunction with coroutines.

The module heading may optionally contain *import* and *export lists.* The import list specifies identifiers declared outside the module but used within it. The export list denotes locally declared identifiers that may be imported by other modules. A module may have several import lists but only one export list.

If the export list is preceded by the reserved word QUALIFIED, it is regarded as a *qualified export.* An importing module must refer to such exported items through *qualified identifiers*, which are formed by prefixing the module's name to the identifer:

```
MODULE M1;
  EXPORT QUALIFIED b;
  VAR
    b : INTEGER;
. . .
END M1;

MODULE M2;
  IMPORT M1;
. . .
  WriteInt(M1.b,Ø);      (* access M1's qualified export *)
END M2;
```

The importing module may *unqualify* an export by including the reserved word FROM with the identifiers to be imported. An example follows:

```
MODULE M2;
  FROM M1 IMPORT b;
. . .
  WriteInt(b,Ø);      (* accessing M1's export needs *)
END M2;              (* no qualification *)
```

All of the identifiers in a module's export list can be imported by importing the module name in the form

```
IMPORT M1;
```

If a RECORD or enumeration type is exported, then all of its field identifiers or constant values are exported, too.

The *module body* is automatically executed before the first call to a local procedure is made.

A module may be split into DEFINITION and IMPLEMENTATION parts contained in independent *compilation units*; this allows interface specifications to be separated from operational details. All declarations in the DEFINITION module are automatically exported. An export list is usually still included, however, for explicit documentation.

IMPLEMENTATION modules encapsulate module declarations, procedure bodies, and module bodies. They may also contain import lists, but not export lists.

A type declaration listed in the DEFINITION part but defined in the IMPLEMENTATION part is called an *opaque export*. Opaque exports hide the details of a type's structure. In the following example, FileKey is an opaque export.

```
DEFINITION MODULE FileHandler;
EXPORT QUALIFIED FileKey,
                 Open;
TYPE
  FileKey;    (* opaque type *)
PROCEDURE Open(VAR f : FileKey;
               name : ARRAY OF CHAR);
END FileHandler.
```

```
IMPLEMENTATION MODULE FileHandler;
TYPE
  FileKey = POINTER TO
            RECORD
                Drive : CARDINAL;
                eof : BOOLEAN;
                BlockNum : CARDINAL;
                NextByte : CARDINAL;
            END;
PROCEDURE Open(VAR f : FileKey;
               name : ARRAY OF CHAR);
```

. . .
END FileHandler.

The only valid operations on opaque variables are assignment, comparisons for equality and inequality, and parameter-passing to the procedures of the implementation module. Opaque exports are further restricted to POINTER types.

A.9 Low-level Facilities

Low-level facilities allow programs to dip into a system's underlying hardware and software for machine-dependent operations. Low-level facilities divide into three parts: module SYSTEM, *type-transfer functions*, and *absolute addressing* of variables.

Module SYSTEM hosts procedures and types for performing low-level operations. Because SYSTEM is actually integral to the compiler—that is, it does not reside in an external library—it is called a *pseudomodule*.

The types exported from SYSTEM are shown in Table A–4.

Table A–4 Types Exported from SYSTEM

Type	Description
ADDRESS	Defined as POINTER TO WORD and compatible with all pointer types and type CARDINAL
PROCESS	Used to declare process variables or *coroutines*
WORD	Represents one storage unit. No operators except assignment apply to type WORD. Formal WORD parameters are compatible with any type of actual paramter occupying one storage unit. (The size of a storage unit is system dependent. On 16-bit computers, a storage unit occupies 16 bits.) If a formal parameter is declared as ARRAY OF WORD, its corresponding actual parameter may be of any type.

The procedures exported from SYSTEM are shown in Table A–5.

Table A–5 Procedures Exported from SYSTEM

Procedure	Description
ADR(x)	Function procedure of type ADDRESS that returns storage address of x
IOTRANSFER(VAR p1, p2 : PROCESS; v : CARDINAL);	Resumes process designated by p2 and saves state of current process in p1. Next processor interrupt occurring through vector number v causes an automatic TRANSFER(p2,p1).
LISTEN	Temporarily lowers a module's priority, allowing any pending IOTRANSFERs to occur
NEWPROCESS(p : PROC; a : ADDRESS; n : CARDINAL; VAR p1 : PROCESS);	Creates new process or coroutine. Parameterless procedure p is the process, a is the base address of the process workspace, n is the size of the workspace, and p1 is the resulting process variable.
SIZE(x)	Function procedure of type CARDINAL that returns number of storage units assigned to variable x
TRANSFER(VAR p1, p2 : PROCESS);	Resumes process designated by p2 and saves state of current process in p1
TSIZE(T)	Function procedure of type CARDINAL that returns number of storage units assigned to type T

Type-transfer functions convert a given parameter into a corresponding value of another type. The type is indicated by the function name. For example, given the declarations

```
VAR
  i : INTEGER;
  b : BOOLEAN;
```

the assignment

    i := INTEGER(b);

interprets the boolean variable b as an integer. No computations are performed; the compiler's type-checking is merely relaxed.

Type transfer is restricted to variables occupying the same number of words in memory.

Variables may be assigned *absolute addresses* in memory by indicating the address in brackets following the identifier name. An example follows:

    VAR
        PortStat[ØFFFH] : BITSET;   (* port status at address
                                           hexadecimal 0FFF *)

B. Standard-module Library

This appendix describes the standard module library of Modula-2. Many implementations may choose to supplement this minimum library with additional modules.

B.1 InOut

InOut contains procedures for performing formatted input and output (I/O) to either the terminal or a file. Input and output are directed to the terminal unless the procedure OpenInput or OpenOutput is called. OpenInput and OpenOutput redirect I/O to files. I/O reverts back to the terminal upon execution of procedures CloseInput and CloseOutput. At most, two files can be open simultaneously: one for input and one for output.

The following statements outline the definition module:

```
DEFINITION MODULE InOut;
    FROM FileSystem IMPORT File;        (* get File management data
                                           structure *)

    EXPORT QUALIFIED
                        (* constant *)
        EOL,            (* end of line character *)
                        (* variables *)
        Done,           (* successful file operation indicator *)
        in,             (* input file management data *)
        out,            (* output file management data*)
        termCH,         (* string terminating character *)
                        (* procedures *)
        OpenInput,      (* open file for input *)
        OpenOutput,     (* open file for output *)
        CloseInput,     (* close input file *)
        CloseOutput,    (* close output file *)
        Read,           (* read a character *)
        ReadString,     (* read a string of characters *)
        ReadInt,        (* read INTEGER value *)
        ReadCard,       (* read CARDINAL value *)
```

```
      Write,            (* write a character *)
      WriteLn,          (* write carriage return and line feed *)
      WriteString,      (* write a string of characters *)
      WriteInt,         (* write INTEGER value *)
      WriteCard,        (* write CARDINAL value *)
      WriteOct,         (* write octal value *)
      WriteHex;         (* write hexadecimal value *)
   CONST
      EOL = 15C;   (* end of line character *)

   VAR
      Done : BOOLEAN;       (* successful file operation indicator,
                               TRUE => success,
                               FALSE => failure *)
      termCH : CHAR;        (* terminating character from
                               ReadString, ReadInt & ReadCard *)
      in,
      out : File;           (* input and output file variables *)
   PROCEDURE OpenInput(defext : ARRAY OF CHAR);
```

(* Accept a file name from the terminal and open it for input. If
   successful, subsequent input is taken from the file instead of
   terminal until CloseInput is called.

      Entry;
         defext = default file extension appended to file name if file
                  name ends with "." (period).

      Exit:
         Done = TRUE, if successful. *)

```
   PROCEDURE OpenOutput(defext : ARRAY OF CHAR);
```

(* Accept a file name from the terminal and open it for output. If
   successful, subsequent output is written to the file instead of
   terminal until CloseOutput is called. If the file already exists, it will
   be overwritten.

      Entry:
         defext = default file extension appended to file name if file
                  name ends with "." (period).

      Exit:
         Done = TRUE, if successful. *)

```
   PROCEDURE CloseInput;
```

(* Close input file and revert to terminal for input. *)

PROCEDURE CloseOutput;
(* Close output file and revert to terminal for output. *)

PROCEDURE Read(VAR ch : CHAR);

(* Read next character from current input. If reading from the
   terminal, the character is not echoed on the screen.
        Exit:
            ch = character read.
            Done = TRUE, if successful,
                    FALSE, if end of file. *)

PROCEDURE ReadString(VAR s : ARRAY OF CHAR);

(* Read string from current input. Leading spaces are ignored. Input
   is terminated by first character <= " " (space). The terminating
   character is assigned to termCH. If reading from the terminal,
   characters are echoed on the screen and backspacing is allowed.
        Exit:
            termCH = terminator.
            s = string read excluding terminator. *)

PROCEDURE ReadInt(VAR x : INTEGER);

(* Read string from current input and convert it to an integer.
   Leading plus or minus sign is optionally accepted. If reading from
   the terminal, characters are echoed on the screen and backspacing
   is allowed for editing.
        Exit:
            x = integer value.
            Done = TRUE, if integer was read. *)

PROCEDURE ReadCard(VAR x : CARDINAL);

(* Read string from current input and convert it to cardinal. If
   reading from the terminal, characters are echoed on the screen and
   backspacing is allowed for editing.
        Exit:
            x = cardinal value.
            Done = TRUE, if cardinal was read. *)

PROCEDURE Write(ch : CHAR);

(* Write a character to current output.
        Entry:
            ch = character to write. *)

PROCEDURE WriteLn;

(* Write a carriage return and line feed to the current output *)

PROCEDURE WriteString(s : ARRAY OF CHAR);

(* Write string to current output.

    Entry:
       s = string to write. *)

PROCEDURE WriteInt(x : INTEGER,
               n : CARDINAL);

(* Convert x to decimal string and write it to current output in field
    size of at least n characters. If x is negative, a leading minus sign
    is included and the minus sign counts as a significant digit. If n is
    greater than the number of significant digits, leading spaces are
    added. If n is zero, only the significant digits are written.

    Entry:
       x = integer decimal value.
       n = minimum field width. *)

PROCEDURE WriteCard(x,
               n : CARDINAL);

(* Convert x to decimal string and write it to current output in field
    size of at least n characters. If n is greater than the number of
    significant digits, leading spaces are added. If n is zero, only the
    significant digits are written.

    Entry:
       x = cardinal decimal value.
       n = minimum field width. *)

PROCEDURE WriteOct(x,
              n : CARDINAL);

(* Convert x to octal string and write it to current output in field size
    of at least n characters. If n is greater than the number of
    significant digits, leading spaces are added. If n is zero, only the
    significant digits are written.

    Entry:
       x = cardinal octal value.
       n = minimum field width. *)

PROCEDURE WriteHex(x,
              n : CARDINAL);

(* Convert x to hexadecimal string and write it to current output in field size of at least n characters. If n is greater than the number of significant digits, leading spaces are added. If n is zero, only the significant digits are written.

    Entry:
      x = cardinal hexadecimal value.
      n = minimum field width. *)

END InOut.

B.2 RealInOut

RealInOut contains procedures for performing formatted input and output (I/O) to either the terminal or a file. These procedures work in conjunction with module InOut. Input and output are directed to the terminal unless the procedure OpenInput or OpenOutput of InOut is called. OpenInput and OpenOutput redirect I/O to files. I/O reverts to the terminal upon execution of procedures CloseInput and CloseOutput.

The following statements outline the definition module:

```
DEFINITION MODULE RealInOut;
  EXPORT QUALIFIED
                    (* variable *)
      Done,             (* successful file operation indicator *)
                    (* procedures *)
      ReadReal,         (* read REAL value *)
      WriteReal,        (* write REAL value *)
      WriteRealOct;     (* write REAL octal value *)
  VAR
    Done : BOOLEAN;    (* successful file operation indicator,
                          TRUE => success,
                          FALSE => failure *)

PROCEDURE ReadReal(VAR x : REAL);
```

(* Read string from current input and convert it to real. Input is
    terminated by first characer <= " " (space). Leading plus or minus
    sign is optionally accepted. If reading from the terminal, characters
    are echoed on the screen and backspacing is allowed for editing.
    Input may be formatted with up to seven significant digits in
    exponential or nonexponential form. If exponential, maximum
    exponent is 38.

      Exit:
        x = real value.
        Done = TRUE, if real was read. *)

PROCEDURE WriteReal(x : REAL;
                    n : CARDINAL);

(* Convert x to decimal string in real, exponential form and write it to current output in field size of at least n characters. If n is greater than the number of significant digits, leading spaces are added. If n is zero, only the significant digits are written.

    Entry:
        x = real decimal value.
        n = minimum field width. *)

PROCEDURE WriteRealOct(x : REAL);

(* Convert x to octal string in real, exponential form and write it to current output.

    Entry:
        x = real octal value. *)

END RealInOut.

B.3 MathLib0

MathLib0 contains function procedures for performing elementary mathematical calculations.

The following statements outline the definition module:

DEFINITION MODULE MathLib0;
EXPORT QUALIFIED
                    (* procedures *)
    sqrt,   (* calculate square root *)
    exp,   (* calculate e to x power *)
    ln,   (* calculate natural logarithm *)

sin,	(* calculate trigonometric sine *)
cos,	(* calculate trigonometric cosine *)
arctan,	(* calculate trigonometric arctangent *)
real,	(* convert integer to real *)
entier;	(* convert real to integer *)

PROCEDURE sqrt(x : REAL) : REAL;
  (* Calculate square root of x (x must be positive). *)

PROCEDURE exp(x : REAL) : REAL;
  (* Raise e to the x power (e is the base of natural logarithms and is
    equal to 2.71828...). *)

PROCEDURE ln(x : REAL): REAL;
  (* Calculate natural logarithm with base e (x must be > 0). If
    exp(x) = y, then ln(y) = x. *)

PROCEDURE sin(x : REAL) : REAL;
  (* Calculate trigonometric sine of x radians.
    For reference, 180 degrees = pi radians (3.141592654 radians)
                    360 degrees = 2 pi radians
                     90 degrees = pi/2 radians *)

PROCEDURE cos(x : REAL) : REAL;
  (* Calculate trigonometric cosine of x radians. *)

PROCEDURE arctan(x : REAL) : REAL;
  (* Calculate trigonometric arctangent of x (angle in radians whose
    tangent is x). *)

PROCEDURE real(i : INTEGER) : REAL;
  (* Convert integer i to real value. *)

PROCEDURE entier(x : REAL) : INTEGER;
  (* Convert real x to integer value. The fractional part of x is
    truncated. *)

END MathLib0.

B.4 Storage

Storage contains procedures for management of dynamic variables. The usual way to handle dynamic variables is to import module Storage and call procedures NEW and DISPOSE, which are automatically translated into calls to procedures ALLOCATE and DEALLOCATE.

The following statements outline the definition module:

```
DEFINITION MODULE Storage;
  FROM SYSTEM IMPORT ADDRESS;
  EXPORT QUALIFIED
                (* procedures *)
    ALLOCATE,      (* allocate storage *)
    DEALLOCATE,    (* deallocate storage *)
    Available;          (* determine if sufficient storage available *)
PROCEDURE ALLOCATE(VAR a : ADDRESS;
                      size : CARDINAL);
(* Allocate dynamic storage indicated by size.
    Entry:
      size = number of bytes to allocate.
    Exit:
      a = ADDRESS of allocated storage. *)

PROCEDURE DEALLOCATE(VAR a : ADDRESS;
                      size : CARDINAL);
(* Deallocate dynamic storage indicated by size.
    Entry:
      size = number of bytes to deallocate.
      a = ADDRESS of storage to be deallocated. *)

PROCEDURE Available(size : CARDINAL) : BOOLEAN;
(* Determine if dynamic storage indicated by variable is available.
    Entry:
      size = number of bytes.
    Exit:
      Available = TRUE, if storage available
                = FALSE, otherwise. *)

END Storage.
```

B.5 FileSystem

Strictly speaking, FileSystem is not one of Modula-2's standard library modules. Most systems include it, however, because it was implemented in the original Modula-2 compiler on the Lilith computer and it provides the only vehicle for random file access. Implementations may vary slightly from the model presented here, so it is best to check the precise definitions and descriptions of the procedures on your system before writing a program that uses FileSystem.

FileSystem treats files as a sequence of characters or words. A character is stored as one byte; a word is stored as two bytes. Access to characters and words occurs relative to the *current position* of the file. After a call to Lookup, Create, or Reset, the current position is set to the file's beginning. Reads and writes automatically increment the current position. Procedure SetPos changes the position to a given value.

The following outlines the definition module of FileSystem:

```
DEFINITION MODULE FileSystem;
  FROM SYSTEM IMPORT ADDRESS,
                      WORD;
  EXPORT QUALIFIED
                          (* types *)
          File,           (* file variable *)
          Response,       (* result of file operation *)
                          (* procedures *)
          Create,         (* create temporary file *)
          Close,          (* terminate file operations *)
          Lookup,         (* search for/create file *)
          Rename,         (* change file name *)
          SetRead,        (* set file to reading state *)
          SetWrite,       (* set file to writing state *)
          SetModify,      (* set file to modifying state *)
          SetOpen,        (* set file to open state *)
          SetPos,         (* set file current position *)
          GetPos,         (* get file current position *)
          Length,         (* return file length *)
          Reset,          (* set file to open & position at beginning *)
          Again,          (* put character in buffer to be read again *)
          ReadWord,       (* read WORD from file current position *)
          WriteWord,      (* write WORD to file current position *)
          ReadChar,       (* read CHAR from file current position *)
          WriteChar;      (* write CHAR to file current position *)

TYPE
  Response = (done,              notdone,
              notsupported,      callerror,
              unknownmedium,     unknownfile,
              paramerror,        toomanyfiles,
              eom,               deviceoff,
              softparityerror,   softprotected,
              softerror,         hardparityerror,
```

                    hardprotected,   timeout,
                    harderror);
File = RECORD
            id : CARDINAL;
            eof : BOOLEAN;   (* end of file indicator *)
            res : Response;
      END;

PROCEDURE Create(VAR f : File;
                     mediumname : ARRAY OF CHAR);

(* Create a temporary unnamed file and set current position to file
   beginning. To make the file permanent, it has to be named with a
   nonnull name through the procedure Rename before closing it. The
   variable mediumname is an unused parameter left over from the
   Lilith.

      Entry:
         mediumname = null string.

      Exit:
         f = initialized file structure
         f.res = done, if operation successful,
            # done, otherwise. *)

PROCEDURE Close(VAR f : File);

(* Terminate operations on file f. If f is temporary, it will be deleted.
      Entry:
         f = structure referencing an initialized file.

      Exit:
         f.res = done, if operation successful,
            # done, otherwise. *)

PROCEDURE Lookup(VAR f : File;
                     filename : ARRAY OF CHAR;
                     new : BOOLEAN);

(* Search for file specified by drive and name given in filename, and
   set current position to beginning of file. If file is found, it is opened
   as file structure f. If file is not found, new is checked. If new is
   TRUE, a new, permanent file with the name given in filename is

created and it is opened as file structure f. If new is FALSE, no action takes place.

> Entry:
>> filename = drive and file name to search.
>> new = TRUE, if file should be created if not found.
>
> Exit:
>> f = initialized file structure
>> f.res = done, if file opened,
>>> = notdone, if file not found & new = FALSE,
>>> # done or notdone, if error. *)

PROCEDURE Rename(VAR f : File;
                       filename : ARRAY OF CHAR);

(* Change name of file f to filename. If filename is a null string, f is changed to a temporary nameless file. If f is a temporary file just initialized by the Create procedure, Rename makes it permanent.

> Entry:
>> f = structure referencing an initialized file.
>> filename = drive and new file name.
>
> Exit:
>> f.res = done, if file renamed,
>>> = notdone, if file with filename already exists,
>>> # done or notdone, if error. *)

PROCEDURE SetRead(VAR f : File);

(* Set the file to reading state without changing the current position.

> Entry:
>> f = structure referencing an initialized file.
>
> Exit:
>> f.res = done, if successful
>>> # done, if error. *)

PROCEDURE SetWrite(VAR f : File);

(* Set the file to writing state without changing the current position.

> Entry:
>> f = structure referencing an initialized file.
>
> Exit:
>> f.res = done, if successful
>>> # done, if error. *)

PROCEDURE SetModify(VAR f : File);

(* Set the file to modifying state without changing the current position.

    Entry:
        f = structure referencing an initialized file.
    Exit:
        f.res = done, if successful
            # done, if error. *)

PROCEDURE SetOpen(VAR f : File);

(* Set the file to open state without changing the current position.

    Entry:
        f = structure referencing an initialized file.
    Exit:
        f.res = done, if successful
            # done, if error. *)

PROCEDURE SetPos(VAR f : File;
                     highpos,
                     lowpos : CARDINAL);

(* Set current file position at

$$(highpos * (2^{16})) + lowpos$$

bytes from the beginning. The new position must be less than or equal to the length of the file.

    Entry:
        f = structure referencing an initialized file.
        highpos = most significant part of position.
        lowpos = least significant part of position.
    Exit:
        f.res = done, if successful
            # done, if error. *)

PROCEDURE GetPos(VAR f : File;
                     VAR highpos,
                     lowpos : CARDINAL);

(* Get current file position. The formula

$$(highpos * (2^{16})) + lowpos$$

indicates position as bytes from file beginning.

    Entry:
        f = structure referencing an initialized file.

Exit:
> highpos = most significant part of position.
> lowpos = least significant part of position. *)

PROCEDURE Length(VAR f : File;
                 VAR highpos,
                     lowpos : CARDINAL);
(* Return file length. The formula

$$(highpos * (2^{16})) + lowpos$$

indicates length in bytes.
> Entry:
>> f = structure referencing an initialized file.
> Exit:
>> highpos = most significant part of length.
>> lowpos = least significant part of length. *)

PROCEDURE Reset(VAR f : File);
(* Set the file to open state and set current position to file beginning.
> Entry:
>> f = structure referencing an initialized file.
> Exit:
>> f.res = done, if successful
>>   # done, if error. *)

PROCEDURE Again (VAR f : File);
(* Return a character to the buffer to be read again. This should be
called after a read operation. It prevents the subsequent read from
reading the next element; the element just read will be returned a
second time. Multiple calls to Again without a read in between have
the same effect as one call. The position in the file is undefined
after a call to Again (it is reset after the next read operation).
> Entry:
>> f = structure referencing an initialized file.
> Exit:
>> f.res = done, if successful
>>   # done, if error. *)

PROCEDURE ReadWord(VAR f : File;
                   VAR w : WORD);

(* Read one word from file at current position. The file will be positioned at the next word when ReadWord is done. If end of file is encountered, w is assigned the value 0C (that is, the character with ordinal number zero).

    Entry:
      f = structure referencing an initialized file.

    Exit:
      w = word read.
      f.eof = TRUE, if read unsuccessful:
              f.res = done, if end of file,
                # done, if error.
         = FALSE, if read successful:
              f.res = done. *)

PROCEDURE ReadChar(VAR f : File;
                      VAR ch : CHAR);

(* Read one character from file at current position. The file will be positioned at the next character when ReadChar is done. If end of file is encountered, ch is assigned the value 0C (that is, the character with ordinal number zero).

    Entry:
      f = structure referencing an initialized file.

    Exit:
      ch = character read.
      f.eof = TRUE, if read unsuccessful:
              f.res = done, if end of file,
                # done, if error.
         = FALSE, if read successful:
              f.res = done. *)

PROCEDURE WriteWord(VAR f : File;
                      w : WORD);

(* Write one word to file at current position. The file will be positioned at the next word when WriteWord is done.

    Entry:
      f = structure referencing an initialized file.
      w = word to be written.

    Exit:
      f.res = done, if successful
         # done, if error. *)

PROCEDURE WriteChar(VAR f : File;
                          ch : CHAR);

(* Write one character to file at current position. The file will be
   positioned at the next character when WriteChar is done.

    Entry:
        f = structure referencing an initialized file.
        ch = character to be written.

    Exit:
        f.res = done, if successful
            # done, if error. *)

END FileSystem.

C. ASCII Character Set

ordinal number			character	ordinal number			character
decimal	*octal*	*hex*		*decimal*	*octal*	*hex*	
0	000	00	nul	17	021	11	dc1
1	001	01	soh	18	022	12	dc2
2	002	02	stx	19	023	13	dc3
3	003	03	etx	20	024	14	dc4
4	004	04	eot	21	025	15	nak
5	005	05	enq	22	026	16	syn
6	006	06	ack	23	027	17	etb
7	007	07	bel	24	030	18	can
8	010	08	bs	25	031	19	em
9	011	09	ht	26	032	1A	sub
10	012	0A	lf	27	033	1B	esc
11	013	0B	vt	28	034	1C	fs
12	014	0C	ff	29	035	1D	gs
13	015	0D	cr	30	036	1E	rs
14	016	0E	so	31	037	1F	us
15	017	0F	si	32	040	20	space
16	020	10	dle	33	041	21	!

ordinal number			character	ordinal number			character
decimal	*octal*	*hex*		*decimal*	*octal*	*hex*	
34	042	22	"	72	110	48	H
35	043	23	#	73	111	49	I
36	044	24	$	74	112	4A	J
37	045	25	%	75	113	4B	K
38	046	26	&	76	114	4C	L
39	047	27	'	77	115	4D	M
40	050	28	(	78	116	4E	N
41	051	29	)	79	117	4F	O
42	052	2A	*	80	120	50	P
43	053	2B	+	81	121	51	Q
44	054	2C	,	82	122	52	R
45	055	2D	−	83	123	53	S
46	056	2E	.	84	124	54	T
47	057	2F	/	85	125	55	U
48	060	30	0	86	126	56	V
49	061	31	1	87	127	57	W
50	062	32	2	88	130	58	X
51	063	33	3	89	131	59	Y
52	064	34	4	90	132	5A	Z
53	065	35	5	91	133	5B	[
54	066	36	6	92	134	5C	\
55	067	37	7	93	135	5D	]
56	070	38	8	94	136	5E	↑
57	071	39	9	95	137	5F	−
58	072	3A	:	96	140	60	`
59	073	3B	;	97	141	61	a
60	074	3C	<	98	142	62	b
61	075	3D	=	99	143	63	c
62	076	3E	>	100	144	64	d
63	077	3F	?	101	145	65	e
64	100	40	@	102	146	66	f
65	101	41	A	103	147	67	g
66	102	42	B	104	150	68	h
67	103	43	C	105	151	69	i
68	104	44	D	106	152	6A	j
69	105	45	E	107	153	6B	k
70	106	46	F	108	154	6C	l
71	107	47	G	109	155	6D	m

ordinal number			character
decimal	*octal*	*hex*	
110	156	6E	n
111	157	6F	o
112	160	70	p
113	161	71	q
114	162	72	r
115	163	73	s
116	164	74	t
117	165	75	u
118	166	76	v
119	167	77	w
120	170	78	x
121	171	79	y
122	172	7A	z
123	173	7B	{
124	174	7C	|
125	175	7D	}
126	176	7E	~
127	177	7F	del

Answers to Selected Problems

Chapter 1

1.1 Strings a, b, c, and d are valid.

1.3 Ada.

Chapter 2

2.1 The following expressions are valid:
```
    b := +9;
    c := −15.88;
    c := c / 3.0;
```

2.3 MODULE FathomsToFeet;   (* Convert fathoms to feet *)
```
    FROM InOut IMPORT WriteLn,
                      WriteString,
                      WriteCard;

    CONST
      FeetInFathom = 6;
    VAR
      NumFeet : CARDINAL;
    BEGIN
      WriteLn;
      WriteString("Converting fathoms to feet");
      WriteLn;
      NumFeet := 2290 * FeetInFathom;
      WriteString("2290 fathoms = ");
      WriteCard(NumFeet,5);
      WriteLn;
      NumFeet := 2043 * FeetInFathom;
      WriteString("2043 fathoms = ");
      WriteCard(NumFeet,5);
      WriteLn;
```

```
     NumFeet := 727 * FeetInFathom;
     WriteString("727 fathoms = ");
     WriteCard(NumFeet,5);
     WriteLn;
END FathomsToFeet.
```

2.5
```
MODULE SampleCalc;      (* Perform calculations *)
FROM InOut IMPORT WriteLn,
                       WriteString;
FROM RealInOut IMPORT WriteReal;
BEGIN
   WriteLn;
   WriteString("Perform calculations");
   WriteLn;
   WriteString("fathoms in 79413 inches = ");
   WriteReal((79413.0 / (12.0 * 6.0)) , 10);
   WriteLn;
   WriteString("meters in one mile = ");
   WriteReal(((5280.0 * 12.0) / 39.37) , 10);
   WriteLn;
   WriteString("speed of sound in miles per second = ");
   WriteReal((1088.0 / 5280.0) , 10);
   WriteLn;
END SampleCalc.
```

Chapter 3

3.1 a. 5

   b. 10

   c. 16

   d. 121

   e. 12500

3.3 The value of the entire expression is determined by the first operand alone in a and c.

Chapter 4

4.1 ArcticTemp is INTEGER.
    MenuSelection is CARDINAL.
    HexDigits is CHAR.

4.2 VAL(suits,3) yields hearts.
    ORD(white) = ORD (i8086) yields TRUE.
    ORD(red) yields 0.

Chapter 5

```
5.1  MODULE Fibonacci;        (* Calculate Fibonacci number *)
     FROM InOut IMPORT WriteLn,
                       WriteString,
                       ReadCard,
                       WriteCard;
     VAR
       n : CARDINAL;       (* input number *)
     PROCEDURE Fib(num : CARDINAL) : CARDINAL;
       BEGIN
         IF (num <= 2) THEN
           RETURN 1;
         ELSE
           RETURN (Fib(num - 1) + Fib(num - 2));
         END;      (* IF *)
       END Fib;
     BEGIN     (* MODULE Fibonacci *)
       WriteLn;
       WriteString("Calculating Fibonacci number ");
       WriteLn;
       WriteString("Enter n: ");
       ReadCard(n);
       WriteCard(Fib(n),5);
       WriteLn;
     END Fibonacci.
```

Chapter 6

6.2 No. Because the type of variable qty is opaque, no operations may be performed on it other than assignment, comparison, and parameter-passing.

Notes

page

xiv   Joseph Moxon, *Mathematicks Made Easie.* Atlas, 1700, page following title page.

4   Definition of structured programming excerpted from Anthony Ralston and Edwin Reilly, *Encyclopedia of Computer Science and Engineering.* (2nd ed.) Van Nostrand Reinhold, 1983, pp. 1444, 1450.

6   Weinberg quote taken from Gerald Weinberg, *The Psychology of Computer Programming.* Van Nostrand Reinhold, 1971, p. 244.

6   Wirth quote taken from Edward Joyce, "The Making of Modula-2." *PC*, vol. 3, no. 6 (April 3, 1984) p. 178.

7   Hoare quotes taken from his article, "The Emperor's Old Clothes." *Communications of the ACM*, vol. 24, no. 2 (February 1981) p. 81

8   Wirth quotes taken from Edward Joyce, "The Making of Modula-2." *PC*, vol. 3, no. 6 (April 3, 1984) p. 178.

8   Ed Post, "Real Programmers Don't Use Pascal." *Datamation,* vol. 29, no. 7 (July 1983) pp. 263–265.

8   "If a language"—Niklaus Wirth, "Design and Implementation of Modula." *Software Practice and Experience 7* (1977).

9   "Modula was never"—from Edward Joyce, "The Making of Modula-2." *PC*, vol. 3, no. 6 (April 3, 1984) pp. 179–180.

9   Lilith photograph reprinted from Siegmund Hurwitz, *Lilith die erste Eva.* Daimon Verlag, AG, 1980, p. 10.

10   Regan quote taken from "Computer Design Pioneers." *Computer Design* (December 1982) p. 77.

11   "In my opinion"—from Edward Joyce, "The Making of Modula-2." *PC*, vol. 3, no. 6 (April 3, 1984) p. 181.

11   "spend all his time"—from Edward Joyce, "The Making of Modula-2." *PC*, vol. 3, no. 6 (April 3, 1984) p. 181.

11   "Nowadays, most"—from Edward Joyce, "The Making of Modula-2." *PC*, vol. 3, no. 6 (April 3, 1984) p. 181.

12   "I don't think"—from "Computer Design Pioneers." *Computer Design* (December 1982) p. 92.

27   Carl Boyer, *A History of Mathematics.* John Wiley and Sons, 1968, pp. 244–245.

45   Tracy Kidder, *The Soul of a New Machine.* Avon, 1982, pp. 89–90.

49–50   Carl Boyer, *A History of Mathematics.* John Wiley and Sons, 1968, pp. 632–634.

79   R. Rivest, A. Shamir and L. Adleman, "A Method for Obtaining Digital Signatures and Public-Key Cryptosystems." *Communications of the ACM*, vol. 21, no. 2 (February 1978) pp. 120–126.

85–86   Glenford Myers, *Software Reliability.* John Wiley and Sons, 1976, pp. 275–276.

165   Wirth quote taken from Niklaus Wirth, *Programming in Modula-2.* (2nd ed.) Springer-Verlag, 1983, p. 80.

191   Maezel Chess Automaton described in "Program Power." *Scientific American*, vol. 244, no. 4 (April 1981) p. 83.

Bibliography and Resources

The following bibliography lists book and magazine references that are cited in this book or are related to Modula-2.

Boyer, C. B. *A History of Mathematics.* John Wiley and Sons, 1968.

Coar, D. "Pascal, Ada, and Modula-2." *Byte*, vol. 9, no. 8 (August 1984) pp. 215—232.

"Computer Design Pioneers." *Computer Design* (December 1982) pp. 76–93.

Cooper, D. and Clancy, M. *Oh! Pascal!* W. W. Norton, 1982.

Gleaves, R. *Modula-2 for Pascal Programmers.* Springer-Verlag, 1984.

Grogono, P. *Programming in Pascal.* (2nd ed.) Addison-Wesley, 1984.

Gutknecht, J. "Tutorial on Modula-2." *Byte*, vol. 9, no. 8 (August 1984) pp. 157–176.

Hoare, C. A. R. "The Emperor's Old Clothes." *Communications of the ACM*, vol. 24, no. 2 (February 1981) pp. 75–83.

Hoppe, J. "A Simple Nucleus Written in Modula-2: A Case Study." *Software Practice and Experience 10* (1980) 697–706.

Jensen, K. and Wirth, N. *Pascal User Manual and Report* (2nd ed.) Springer-Verlag, 1976.

Joyce, E. J. "The Making of Modula-2." *PC*, vol. 3, no. 6 (April 3, 1984) pp. 176–181.

Joyce, E. J. "Modula-2 for Pascal Programmers." *PC*, vol. 3, no. 6 (April 3, 1984) pp. 193–197.

Joyce, E. J. "A $40 Invitation to Modula-2." *PC*, vol. 3, no. 6 (April 3, 1984) pp. 183–186.

Joyce, E. J. "Modula-2: Son of Pascal." *Microcomputing*, vol. 8, no. 8 (August 1984) pp. 70–74.

Joyce, E. J. "Volition's Modula-2 on the Sage." *Byte*, vol. 9, no. 10 (September 1984) pp. 351–353.

Joyce, E. J. "Logitech's New Breed of Modula-2." *Microcomputing,* vol. 8, no. 10 (October 1984) pp. 62–66.

Kidder, J. T. *The Soul of a New Machine.* Avon, 1982.

McCormack, J. and Gleaves, R. "Modula-2." *Byte,* vol. 8, no. 4 (April 1983) pp. 385–395.

Moxon, J. *Mathematicks Made Easie.* Atlas, 1700.

Myers, G. J. *Software Reliability.* John Wiley and Sons, 1976.

Ohran, R. "Lilith and Modula-2." *Byte,* vol. 9, no. 8 (August 1984) pp. 181–192.

Paul, R. J. "An Introduction to Modula-2." *Byte,* vol. 9, no. 8 (August 1984) pp. 195–210.

Post, E. "Real Programmers Don't Use Pascal." *Datamation,* vol. 29, no. 7 (July 1983) pp. 263–265.

Pournelle, J. "User's Column: Ulterior Motives, Lobo, Buying Your First Computer, JRT Update." *Byte,* vol. 8, no. 5 (May 1983) pp. 298–324.

Ralston, A. and Reilly, Jr., E. D. *Encyclopedia of Computer Science and Engineering.* (2nd ed.) Van Nostrand Reinhold, 1983.

Rivest, R. L., Shamir, A., and Adleman, L. "A Method for Obtaining Digital Signatures and Public-Key Cryptosystems." *Communications of the Association for Computing Machinery,* vol. 21, no. 2 (February 1978) pp. 120–126.

Spector, D. "Lexing and Parsing Modula-2." *SIGPLAN Notices,* vol. 18, no. 10 (October 1983) pp. 25–32.

Strehlo, K. "Modula-2 Moves from the Lab to the Market." *Mini-Micro Systems* (May 1982) pp. 153–156.

Weinberg, G. M. *The Psychology of Computer Programming.* Van Nostrand Reinhold, 1971.

Welsh, J., Sneeringer, W. J., and Hoare, C. A. R. "Ambiguities and Insecurities in Pascal." *Software Practice and Experience 7* (1977) pp. 685–696.

Wirth, N. and Hoare, C. A. R. "A Contribution to the Development of ALGOL." *Communications of the ACM,* vol. 9, no. 6 (June 1966) pp. 413–432.

Wirth, N. *Algorithms + Data Structures = Programs.* Prentice-Hall, 1976.

Wirth, N. "Modula: A Language for Modular Multiprogramming." *Software Practice and Experience 7* (1977) 3–35.

Wirth, N. "The Use of Modula." *Software Practice and Experience 7* (1977) pp. 37–66.

Wirth, N. "Design and Implementation of Modula." *Software Practice and Experience 7* (1977) pp. 67–84.

Wirth, N. *Programming in Modula-2.* (2nd ed.) Springer-Verlag, 1983.

Wirth, N. "History and Goals of Modula-2." *Byte,* vol. 9, no. 8 (August 1984) pp. 145–152.

Wirth, N. "From Programming Language Design to Computer Construction." *Communications of the Association for Computing Machinery,* vol. 28, no. 2 (February 1985) pp. 159–164.

Resources

Distributors of Modula-2 Compilers

Hochstrasser Computing AG
Chratzstrasse 14
8954 Geroldswil
Switzerland

Hochstrasser sells a compiler for Z80 CP/M systems.

Institut fuer Informatik
Eidgenoessiche Technische Hochschule (ETH)
CH–8092
Zurich, Switzerland

The Swiss Federal Institute of Technology (ETH) distributes the PDP-11 source code for the original Modula-2 compiler developed by Niklaus Wirth. The source code costs $160.

Interface Technologies Corp.
3336 Richmond
Houston, TX 77098
713–523–8422

Interface sells a Modula-2 development system for the IBM PC.

Logitech, Inc.
805 Veterans Blvd.
Redwood City, CA 94063
415–365–9852

Logitech sells compilers for MS-DOS and CP/M-86 systems.

Maritime Infosystems Ltd.
6660 Reservoir Rd.
Corvalis, OR 97333
503–929–2552

Maritime sells a compiler for the 68000 microprocessor.

Modula Research Institute (MRI)
950 N. University Ave.

MRI sells compilers for MS-DOS systems. MRI also distributes the PDP-11 source code for the original Modula-2 compiler developed by Niklaus Wirth. The source code costs $160.

Modula Corporation
950 N. University Ave.
Provo, UT 84604
801–375–7400

Modula Corporation sells compilers for MS-DOS systems and the Apple II, Lisa, and Macintosh computers. The company also sells the Lilith computer and Pascal-to-Modula-2 converters.

Pinnacle Systems
10410 Markison Road
Dallas, TX 75238
214–340–4941

Pinnacle sells a compiler for the 68000 microprocessor.

Scenic Computer Systems Corp.
14852 N.E. 31st Circle
Redmond, WA 98502
206–885–5500

Scenic sells a compiler for the 68000 microprocessor.

TDI Software Ltd.
10410 Markison Rd.
Dallas, TX 75238
214–340–4942

TDI sells a compiler for Atari computers.

Modula-2 User Groups

Modula-2 Users Association (MODUS)
c/o Pacific Systems Group
P.O. Box 51778
Palo Alto, CA 94303

Membership fee: $20 per year

Modula-2 Special Interest Group (SIG)
USUS (UCSD Pascal System Users' Society)
P.O. Box 1148
La Jolla, CA 92038

Membership fee: $25 per year

Magazines

Journal of Pascal, Ada & Modula-2
John Wiley & Sons
605 Third Ave.
New York, NY 10157
201–342–6707

Index

Other books in the Microcomputer Books Series are available from your local book or computer store. For more information, write:

Addison-Wesley Publishing Co., Inc.
Microcomputer Books & Consumer Software
Reading, MA 01867
(617) 944–3700

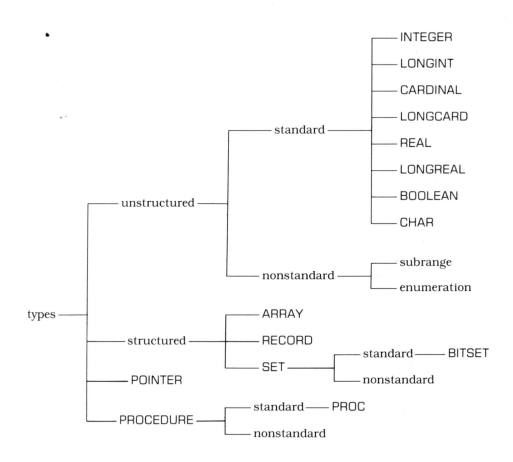

```
types ─┬─ unstructured ─┬─ standard ──────┬─ INTEGER
       │                │                 ├─ LONGINT
       │                │                 ├─ CARDINAL
       │                │                 ├─ LONGCARD
       │                │                 ├─ REAL
       │                │                 ├─ LONGREAL
       │                │                 ├─ BOOLEAN
       │                │                 └─ CHAR
       │                └─ nonstandard ───┬─ subrange
       │                                  └─ enumeration
       │
       ├─ structured ───┬─ ARRAY
       │                ├─ RECORD
       │                └─ SET ──┬─ standard ── BITSET
       │                         └─ nonstandard
       │
       ├─ POINTER
       │
       └─ PROCEDURE ────┬─ standard ── PROC
                        └─ nonstandard
```

Operator Precedence

first (highest)	NOT ~
second	* / DIV MOD AND &
third	+ − OR
fourth (lowest)	= # <> < <= > >= IN